THE
SIGNS
♈ IN ♉
LOVE

**An Interactive Cosmic Road Map
to Finding Love That Lasts**

CAROLYNE FAULKNER

A TarcherPerigee Book

"Lovers don't finally meet somewhere;
they are in each other all along."

—Rumi

tarcherperigee

An imprint of Penguin Random House LLC
penguinrandomhouse.com

Artwork and illustrations by Adrian McCrickard, Carolyne Faulkner, and
Danielle Johnston for D/A London

Most TarcherPerigee books are available at special quantity discounts for bulk
purchase for sales promotions, premiums, fund-raising, and educational needs.
Special books or book excerpts also can be created to fit specific needs. For
details, write: SpecialMarkets@penguinrandomhouse.com.

Trade paperback ISBN: 9780593538616
Ebook ISBN: 9780593538623

Printed in the United States
1st Printing

Book design by Silverglass Studio

Contents

Contents

Contents

Introduction

Love possesses not nor would it be possessed;
For love is sufficient unto love.
—Kahlil Gibran, **The Prophet**

Two strangers can fall in love the moment their eyes meet—because it's not the first time their *souls* have met. These unforgettable encounters rarely are due to chance. Real love spans lifetimes, not years or decades, and is beyond our concept of linear time. Understanding this is freeing.

This little book is a result of my own search for meaning among the debris of one of the strangest, most unpredictable collective experiences in modern times. After many conversations with those far wiser than me, I concluded that our world needs more love, and the only solution is to *be* love. That means starting where we are, and making all our moves with kindness and compassion as the silent drivers. Writing this book helped me resuscitate my own heart, and I sincerely hope it benefits you, too. There has been so much dark, but let's also remember the light, and how exhilarating it feels when we join forces and love each other.

If you're reading this, you probably just want to know about your romantic compatibilities—and you will find that information in abundance in the following pages. But first, take stock of your own ability to raise your consciousness, knowing that what you decide to do today, a million other people may do tomorrow, and every thought you have and decision you make has an impact. We have infinite potential, and we can make a difference just by being more aware, moment by moment, of how amazing it feels when we respond thoughtfully to everything and everyone around us. To achieve real happiness and a lasting sense of contentment, it's time we put our own needs on the back burner and think about the effect we have on others, for better and for worse.

It has never been truer: if all we need is love, the answer is to be love—without condition.

The Signs in Love reveals how, why, and largely what tends to happen when the signs combine and begin that electrifying dance known as falling in love. Whether you step to the beat of a rumba, slow and sensual like water signs; sidestep each other with a playful tango, like air; or flow with the rise and fall of the perfectly timed waltz, like the earth signs, this is all about that initial starry-eyed attraction and each union's potential—and, of course, its pitfalls. This book is written in layers so you get to choose how far to go within the pages and, indeed, within yourself. When you highlight the more profound lessons of your past and present relationships, it deepens the unions you already have, attracts and strengthens the ones you want, and dissolves the pain of past hurts that only hold you back from dancing freely with your soul mate.

As a professional astrologer, I'm repeatedly asked, "Which sign would be my best match?" I explain repeatedly that: (a) people are more complex than the zodiac; (b) the signs interact in different ways based on how the elements (air, fire, water, earth) are balanced within each person and how the elements combine as a couple; and (c) there is no such thing as one sign being totally incompatible with another. Some matches are more challenging than others, but you just have to work a little harder to understand those strengths and the stumbling blocks. Every relationship we have, both personal and professional, requires compromise and subtle yet constant (re)negotiation to prevail. My method, Dynamic Astrology™, offers a tried and tested yet loose framework rather than a prescriptive and definitive road map. In this book I share what I tell my clients about love, the signs, compatibility, and how to guard against unhealthy attachments, which better prepares you for the roller-coaster ride of uncertainty that comes when you love another person.

Much of what I've written is part of a lifelong practice for me, too. I am learning, along with you, about how different everyday life can be when love is considered first, before we act or react. Only then do we manage to defuse anger, negativity, and fear and instead come from a place of loving-kindness. Unless you are blessed with the patience of a saint (and I am not!), it's all too easy to let people get under your skin. When you do manage to win over difficult or negative folk and transform the encounter into something beautiful, it's incredibly gratifying.

This book was created to trigger light-bulb moments of recognition of your unhelpful patterns and to give you the support to alter your attitude toward all your relationships. To attract and retain a suitable life partner or soul mate, you first must be in the right place yourself. Only then are you able to recognize them and transcend that often-fleeting passionate love to something incredible that endures. When you embrace the dance of love and all its chaotic potential, your daily life becomes more poetry in motion and less reenactment of a Shakespeare tragedy. Understanding your own patterns in life and love—what's flowing well and also not so well—unlocks the potential to genuinely align with another and then build something monumental.

Why are some unions destined to last forever and others for only a season? We all know that the former takes compassion, communication, and equal amounts of compromise. Beyond that, it's your own soul that gives you the answers, and its quiet inner voice is hard to hear above the din of a busy life and chattering mind. When we learn to take refuge in stillness—or better still, silence—we can discern the polarity between fantasy and reality. Reality isn't harsh; reality is beautiful because it leads to tangible results that last far beyond one lifetime.

In the search for answers, I realized that love is the only emotion that has the capacity to truly evolve humanity. So know this, dear reader: adopting any of the practices and reflections in these pages will help you not only in your quest for the right union(s), or to maintain the one(s) you may already have, but also to become a more considerate person in general, which is such a beneficial contribution to society. Start where you are, and act moment by moment, day by day. If you start by increasing your own tender, heartfelt vibes, you'll become more loving as a human being. It takes only one light to illuminate the darkness; may you be that light in all you do.

———

Whatever you feel or have heard about astrology, consider perhaps there *is* a binding force that makes certain signs magnetize to each other and successfully hold their commitment for many lifetimes. There is no question that certain unions create different results and reactions between two people, for good and for bad. Some say it's written in the stars, hidden within the secrets of our karma, or a past-life soul connection that defies logic—or perhaps it's a chemical reaction between two people, the sort that causes sparks to crackle and rationale to fly out the window. Here's what I think: as with all matter in the universe, we are made of stardust, so it's not beyond the realms of possibility to analyze love and compatibility based on combined astrology, or synastry. Some unions are explosive and destructive, like neutron stars formed from collapsing giant stars. From that chaos, new stars are born. If certain stars and signs in combination have a signature chemical reaction, they also offer the opportunity to be reborn—and from there, a new story begins.

You can determine the type of connection you have or are perhaps prone to attract. More importantly, you can work to heal past hurts and break unhelpful habits with the self-awareness to embrace the present. Perhaps you can then prevent yourself from incessantly going through the same jarring process as neutron stars.

We are captivated by tales of love at first sight, and we are inspired by stories of people whose love endures the stormy seas of life. Most people still hold onto the hope that one day they will stop the endless loop of unsuitable relationships or overcome past heartache and loss, finally find the one, and live happily ever after. Yes, that thunderbolt of surety happens, and it's real. It's not always indicative of *real* love as opposed to transient desire—one is solid, and the other disintegrates the minute any work is required. However, every relationship (the good, the bad, and the ugly!) offers unparalleled opportunity for personal growth. Absolute honesty and commitment are required of both people to form a partnership strong enough to weather any and all storms. The world is full of optimistic romantics, which means that our perceptions of love and logic rarely combine. That is where this book may offer valuable insight and practical tips to overcome the misunderstandings that arise between people who seemingly come from different universes.

What Is Love?

When I learned that the Sanskrit language has ninety-six words to describe love and English only has one, I presumed that's because in the West, we have a more laissez-faire, consumeristic attitude toward love. We are sold a glamorous fantasy of how our relationships ought to be and too often throw them away if we think they no longer serve us, they are past the "sell by" date, or we seek a "hit" somewhere else the moment we have to face our own not-so-attractive behaviors. Thankfully, our throwaway habits are starting to wane, which is positively impacting our collective attitude toward intimacy, too, as we are far more inclined to try to resolve issues or fix what breaks.

Our world is kept in sync by loving-kindness. It binds us together as a building block of humanity and both steadies and rocks our world with its magic. I always use the phrase "Think with your heart," meaning that if you open your eyes to see and use your heart to feel, you'll find that love is everywhere, with the capacity to transform almost anything, or anyone, into light. When we love and feel loved, our hearts open like flowers basking in the warm glow of the sun. Of course, there are those who have closed their hearts or become unkind or miserly with their affection for one reason or another. These people often fear being taken advantage of or stubbornly refuse to salve the burn of past betrayals, pain, or disappointment. Luckily, it is not too difficult to open a closed heart; you just need to persevere with patience and unconditional love.

You may want to read this book with a journal and pencil in hand to take notes on your findings for later contemplation. These reflections can lead to insightful revelations and empowering transformations. Throughout you'll find exercises labeled "Love Notes." These are an opportunity for you to interact with your thoughts and memories. As you change and grow, so will your notes. Try not to overthink; just start writing.

Try this for starters:

✧ Close your eyes and breathe slowly and restoratively three times. Note the calmness washing over you, and take this with you into your daily life. Inhale and hold your breath while you visualize love and light filling your whole body. The exhale is more important: as you release your breath, imagine light and love encompassing you and maybe another person.

✧ Now repeat the practice, sending the love to your friends and family.

✧ Now try it with your whole neighborhood and, if you're feeling magnanimous, the whole world.

✧ How does it feel when you do this?

✧ Jot down your feelings after each exercise. Journaling is quite effective, and making notes will help you recall this simple method throughout your daily life.

———

Before we begin this journey together, ask yourself honestly if you are ready to face yourself and take your perception of love to a whole new level. I ask this question because some people are far too attached to the past, which wastes precious opportunities in the present. We *can* change the world by releasing blame, forgiving hurts, and opening our hearts, beginning in our daily lives and in being more aware of how we operate. Then and only then can we lead by example.

First, let's start with you, your love relationships to date, and those you wish to usher in.

Let's talk about love.

Do you perceive love to be a risky business?

✧ Ponder that, without some level of risk, there can be no great gain. It's only a negative risk if you are attached to the outcome or don't want to lose face, which isn't speaking from your heart at all.

✧ Jot down times when you were too fearful of losing face to be loving.

✧ When you are faced with anger or unkindness, what's your default setting? How do you usually respond?

✧ Now think of one specific instance, and try the following exercise: try hard to breathe back into the most recent moment of anger you can remember, and pump love into that situation, person, or negativity. If it was your own anger, explore your triggers and jot them down.

✧ When you are faced with an angry neighbor, driver, or colleague, how do you think you respond?

✧ Now recall one instance in which you remained patient and kind.

✧ And now think of one in which you didn't react well.

✧ Revisit both outcomes, and note how you felt after each.

———

When dealing with someone who isn't exactly lovable, always try to hit pause and empathize first. We have no idea what is going on for any other person, so try imagining their suffering before you react. Then follow the rule of three (Ro3).

The Rule of Three

I n any uncomfortable or negative situation, try to respond with patience and kindness. I know it's hard. I find it often takes three attempts to break through fear-fueled anger or unkindness—our own or another's. But it does work. So don't give up; try again if you have to and then once more. You can direct love and empathy to yourself or toward another—or both at once.

Here's how. In a situation when the temperature is rising, take a moment to surround your heart with love and then, in your mind, send loving energy to another. Fighting fire with fire will end in a defeat, so break through with the Ro3. With patience, this magic works wonders, but watch out for your own attachment to fast results or some sort of recognition. I can't always make it happen, either. But when I do manage it, I dance inside and bask in the sunbeams of love.

Let's say your partner is being snippy with you. Instead of reacting defensively, try to respond mindfully three times—the Ro3:

1. Don't react or take anything personally. Instead, take a few measured breaths to ground yourself and silently send the other person love and kindness.
2. Empathize with them, put yourself in their shoes, and try to figure out why they are acting out.
3. Gently ask them three times if they truly mean what they say or do, and only listen to what they respond the third time.

❖ Jot down times when you have applied the rule of three.

❖ And the results?

❖ Even if you seemingly failed, how did trying make you feel?

❖ If you felt good, that's your higher mind speaking. If you felt vulnerable, that's your ego. You were attached to the reward. Forgive yourself and try harder next time.

PART 1

The Connections and Attractions

During my many years as a performance coach and an astrologer, I have often found myself needing to dispel unhelpful myths and fixed beliefs surrounding astrological compatibility—particularly misconceptions that certain signs are not well matched and may lack the compatibility required for a relationship to flourish. I am not saying that there isn't a little truth in the reported difficulties between certain signs, but that is just one part of a much bigger picture. And it's not just about matching star signs either; you need to investigate the natal charts of both individuals to discover how some, or all, of the signs and planets interact. It doesn't have to be complicated, and it's been my life's mission to simplify this process. If you draw both charts and look for the same or opposite sign matches—and not just the (Sun) signs—you will have plenty to work with. If you are ready to jump in, jot down the matches you find by sign and then do some research about those signs and symbols. You can find my guide at dynamicastrology.com.

Again, there is *no such thing* as *incompatibility between signs*. Some matches are more challenging than others, but there will always be a point of connection in the combined full charts that sparked the attraction in the first place. These unions encourage us to grow on a soul level by examining our own actions and reactions honestly and by keeping our hearts open, which is the ultimate talisman.

———

All issues we face in life are due to our attachments—our own and others' expectations, what we think we should be doing, how relationships ought to look, what others think of us, and so on—it can be exhausting! A fixed attitude about the "right" or "wrong" astrological match is just another attachment we should leave behind. It's too generic, and no human is as simple as a sign.

Love Notes

✧ How do others perceive you?

✧ Who do you think you are?

✧ Do the two match?

✧ Now consider how much of those perceptions are real, whatever that means to you. Do you play to your audience or operate in certain ways because others expect it?

✧ What attracts you to another person? Be honest—this is just between you and your soul.

✧ Initially, what makes you decide to form a union?

✧ Ultimately, what makes you want to remain or sever ties?

✧ What do you think others find attractive about you?

✧ How much of this is ego, or worldly, based?

✧ How much of what you have noted comes from your soul or higher mind?

Our Love Affair with Romance

Who among us has never experienced passionate love, with its all-consuming, blazing flames? We sometimes know when we are about to get scorched, but by then it's too late. Even the lows of love, its agony and anguish, serve as great teachers and have inspired some of the world's most exquisite forms of art. From pain repurposed often comes beauty. And to this rush of adrenaline, we often become addicts.

We adore hearing stories and fables about love. Love astrology is much more than just your Sun sign, but this is a good place to begin. After that, for a more holistic understanding, I recommend that you get to know your own stars by calculating your own natal chart and then your love interest's.

A natal, or birth, chart is a map of the positions of certain stars and planets at the time of someone's birth. When you combine two charts to determine the compatibility of a relationship, it's called a synastry chart. Although a synastry chart offers plenty of clues and insights, and is interesting to read, nothing is ever set in stone. *We* are masters of our destinies. How we relate to others is down to us, too. Only by knowing yourself can you see behind someone else's protective mask—truly *see* them—and allow them to see you, and love you, in return. This is the only way to form an authentic, lasting union.

✧ List a few relationships, romantic, platonic, or professional, that went through the following process: you *formed* and all was well, aka the "honeymoon" period, but then you *stormed*, and argued or had a disagreement.

✧ How many of these storms disintegrated or destroyed the relationships?

✧ If you can list more than three, contemplate any running themes. Can you find a common denominator?

✧ Why did the storm devastate the union?

✧ Forget blame and instead ask: what role did you play, both in the initial stages and in the finale?

✧ Did any of these unions break through the barriers and enable you to *really* come together and perform as a couple, or friends, or both?

✧ Note what it was about this person that made you work harder to sustain the union.

✧ What was it about you, or where you were in your own journey?

It's critical to let go of feelings of powerlessness. Stand confident in the knowledge that who you *can* become is all that counts. This life is only a drop in the ocean, so your "age" matters not. Any progress you make toward self-knowledge will stand you in good stead for the rest of your life, and for the many that will follow.

Connections + Attractions

We all have a little of each sign in our full natal charts, which is why there will always be some sort of a match in a synastry chart that gives rise to an interaction. It could be a fire match—exciting, dynamic, and passionate. It may be a water connection—emotional and transformative—or an air sign match, which is cerebral and intoxicating. Or it could be an earth match—healing and grounding for both people. But some connections are more potent than others.

Sun sign connections help us shine in our lives and in our unions, but the Sun in our chart also symbolizes our ego, which we need to face and work to demote to experience real love. So if you have a Sun connection, think closely about this aspect. How do you interact? Is there any level of pretense or showing off? Do you try to impress each other in unhealthy ways?

Venus and Mars connections—if there aren't other significant points of overlap—may mean that the union will fizzle after the chemistry has worn off and any issues can no longer be resolved in the bedroom.

Saturn connections make you put in the work to commit. They're the glue through problematic times. Saturn combined with any other planet can feel restrictive, cold, and austere—or just boring.

The Moon and the North and South Nodes of the Moon, in any combination, indicate a reconnection in this life to rectify mistakes of past lifetimes and to redress karmic imbalances. North Node is about destiny in this life, and South Node indicates where we have been. Both can feel like fate, which means they may drag us back into unhelpful habits and patterns we had managed to kick.

Moon connections result in all-consuming and emotional relationships, but if one person, or both, lacks emotional maturity, these unions can be explosive and destructive, simmering with misunderstandings and pain. Sometimes one person becomes defensive and insecure or takes on the parental role that the other lacked as a child. This is neither balanced nor sexy.

If it's not clear yet, charts are useful pointers, but they are not 100 percent definitive. Compatibility depends on how much the partners have already grown, their levels of emotional maturity, and their souls. In some cases, the issues that show up in synastry charts already have been dissipated in previous unions so they do not play out anymore. Again, it's all down to self-awareness and emotional maturity. All unions, not only in love, need to go through the same process before they solidify: they form, they storm, and then, with clear boundaries established, they perform in a more considerate and respectful manner.

Many of the successful pairings I know of are not actually connected via their Sun signs, but instead through some other sign or planet, whether that's opposite signs, or Moon signs, Saturn to Saturn, etc. Astrological matches can be more intricate than simply the same or opposite signs. Through years of study and experience, I have found that same-sign matches can be powerful conjunctions with the potential to be very harmonious. Opposite signs may hold the same power and potential for transformation and growth as "squares" (see page 275) and, of course, other oppositions, although squares and oppositions are usually the least comfortable!

If you're feeling a bit lost in some of this jargon, that's understandable. But keep reading. This book will introduce you to each of the signs, show you how they connect, and explain how they work, for better and for worse, to help you become a more grounded and receptive partner. It's not just about finding the right one; it's about working hard to *be* the right one. The rest will follow naturally.

Opposites Attract

THE OPPOSITE SIGNS:

Aries–Libra

Taurus–Scorpio

Gemini–Sagittarius

Cancer–Capricorn

Leo–Aquarius

Virgo–Pisces

Opposites indeed attract and are learning comparable lessons, specifically how to overcome similar wounds from different perspectives. They also are learning how to transcend behavioral tendencies that don't serve them, let alone others. It's useful to read your own sign as well as your opposite sign if you want to recognize your own behavior and go-to habits when seeking, pursuing, or being in love.

How It Works

You can use this book to read about how your Sun sign matches with the other zodac signs, or, if you know your natal chart and the natal chart of your partner, friend, or love interest, you will see that the findings relate to any planet connecting to your Sun or your other signs. Remember that it's not always just about a Sun sign match; your partner's zodiac sign may match your rising sign, or your Venus sign may match your love interest's Mars sign, and so on.

Turn to page 53 to read about each sign's relationship to the others and learn how they relate to any matching planet you have in your full chart. Each love match has a light side and a shadow side—I call this "gone wrong" or "gone right," or "flowing well" or "not flowing so well." Neither category is fixed, and just because something went wrong or wasn't flowing in one moment doesn't mean it cannot be transformed in the next. This takes work, self-reflection, and honesty.

Match Your Planets—Fast Track

If you already have both your natal charts, this section explains how to look for signs that match and how they play out. If you don't yet have your charts, draw both of them on dynamicastrology.com or a similar website. You don't necessarily need the exact time of birth to check for major planets, but it helps give you more detailed info. Then, look to the following sections for a translation of your potential as a couple. This fast track shows how your match is *likely* to play out. Remember, it's not black and white. Life isn't fixed or predetermined, and pretending otherwise would disempower you and your choices, which would be bad karma for me and unwise for you. Instead, let's translate the astrology as a reflective tool for empowerment.

The Sun: "Inspirational Love"

Fortune and love favor the brave.
—Ovid

A connection to your Sun sign usually indicates a mighty union and results in a mutual love of life and an appreciation for fun, which yields happiness and expands the heart. This connection has the potential to bring out the best in both of you and help each of you become stronger as a result.

("To Be") Flowing Right: You become more confident, experience happiness and contentment, summon love and bring joy wherever you go, and shine with the brightness of the sun—both individually and as a couple.

("Not Meant to Be") Not Flowing Right: Also known as "pulling an Icarus"—the Sun can burn us by overinflating egos within a selfish union based on superficiality. This combination could expand one or both of your egos in unhelpful ways, such as caring more about how the relationship looks to others than how it really is, or what you or they can get out of it rather than what either or both can give.

◇ Try hard to see your partner and appreciate them for who they are as an individual, as opposed to an extension of yourself. If you are experiencing the unhelpful traits of this union, focus on your partner's appealing characteristics. Review your motivation for being in the relationship and what attracted you in the first place.

◇ Why did you get together, or why do you want to get together?

◇ Was the attraction love for them? What do you, or did you, love about them?

◇ Try to focus on the sincere traits you love, which helps magnify them. What did, or do, they bring to your life, and vice versa?

◇ If you are experiencing Sun connections flowing well, then shine on.

The Moon: "Emotional Love"

The Moon is the intuitive nurturer of the zodiac, evoking kindness without condition. A connection to your Moon sign often results in an emotional and comforting union, a love of intimacy and feeling. It also indicates that you probably have a recent past-life connection.

Flowing Right: Your inner needs are being met, and you feel seen and heard. This union boosts emotional security and enhances emotional intelligence, allowing both of you the safety to be generous and feel supported and cherished, resulting in a balanced partnership with both parties sensitive to the other's needs.

Not Flowing Right: Moon connections indicate hypersensitivity and defensiveness, which lead to miserly behavior, meanness, misunderstandings, and chaos as one or both of you overreacts and takes every word and action as an attack or slight. One partner may attempt to control the other by shutting them down with volatile, angry outbursts.

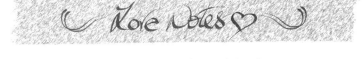

✧ Empathize with your partner, and understand that this is an emotional past-life union. Be patient if you are experiencing the unhelpful traits. They may not have your maturity, so encourage yourself, or them, to get professional help in the form of therapy or anger management.

✧ Are you prone to overreacting? If yes, examine your triggers and get some help.

✧ Do you offer kindness with conditions? If yes, then it's not true kindness, which is unconditional. If no, you are a boss! Teach by example.

✧ If you are experiencing the Moon's connections flowing well, then carry on in all your emotional curiosity and quest for growth.

Mercury: "Cerebral Love"

A connection to your Mercury sign results in a mutual curiosity for life and a thirst for knowledge, indicating shared interests, philosophies, and an electrifying meeting of the minds (unless in an opposition, which means you are likely to learn without necessarily agreeing or thinking similarly). You are both adept in the art of communication, like listening and intuiting.

Flowing Right: You appreciate each other's knowledge and overall intelligence and probably share and debate for hours on end. Mercury aspects can result in an almost telepathic connection (especially with air signs), as each partner seemingly knows how the other's mind works. This can feel like a meeting of the higher minds. Quick-witted Mercury refuses to entertain boredom, often resulting in a similar sense of humor that keeps the union alive even through tough times.

Not Flowing Right: This pairing can sometimes feel negative and superficial, with one or both of you leaning in to ignorance, gossip, or harmful associations. One or both partners can use their talent for words to bring down the other person or wound them with harsh jokes and a biting precision. When not in its flow, Mercury connections may trigger infidelity, deceit, and a lifelong relationship with lies.

✧ You cannot change another person; you only can change how you react, how you are, and how you think. Rise above shallow associations to seek intelligent partners who will enhance your own wisdom. Be kind to yourself and your lovers and know that Mercury connections often are sent to help you face your own shadow side and work on your own mind.

✧ Are you, or is your significant other, prone to fabrications when it comes to your lives and relationship? Do you exaggerate or withhold information? If yes, examine the reasons why.

✧ Do you enjoy listening as much as talking? If yes, Mercury is working well because the planet loves learning.

✧ Are you true to yourself? To others? If not, examine why and vow to work with compassion and truth.

✧ If you are experiencing Mercury's connections flowing well, then carry on as you are, smarty pants.

Venus: "Aspirational Love"

A connection with Venus often results in an almost instant connection, usually to one or the other's beauty. (I say *almost* because instant physical attractions fall to the realm of Mars.) The influence of the planet of love can make you feel that you've found someone who fits your romantic aspirations. You inspire each other to reach for the stars and support each other's goals. Venus connections can help you work toward becoming the right person and partner and heal wounds from past associations and previous loves.

Shared interests in the arts, architecture, and literature are all Venus-ruled pastimes that often find expression here, as well as a love for meeting new people, entertaining, socializing, beautiful spaces, and animals.

Flowing Right: You appreciate the benefits of being in a partnership or union. This flavor of love has the power to regenerate itself if it ever lacks luster. You each aspire to keep the love alive and put in the work to maintain it. Depending on the sign Venus falls in, you also may feel wondrous harmony and destiny.

Not Flowing Right: This might look like a fast love affair that burns out as soon as one sees the other as anything other than a god or goddess. If you put your relationship on a pedestal, then the union will die the moment the picture-perfect image fades.

Love Notes

❖ Aim to bring reality, balance, and harmony to this union while staying true to your needs so each partner is aware of the other's expectations. Be sure your souls are as attractive and attracted as you are to each other's outer appearance.

✧ What was or is the attraction?

✧ Is it based primarily on the physical?

✧ Do you have high expectations of yourself?

✧ What are they?

✧ What do you expect in or from a partner?

✧ If you are experiencing Venus connections flowing well, then carry on as you are, inspiring us all with your beautiful soul.

Mars: "Physical Love"

A connection to your Mars sign often results in a charged and instant physical attraction, making both parties keen to further explore the union. Passionate enthusiasm ensues, as well as energy boosts and the drive to get stuff done. The steaming sexual attraction can become combative if the passion wears off or no positive outlet is found, such as lively joint projects or working out together.

Flowing Right: You possess a dazzling ability to execute projects and deal with issues that may have been challenging in past unions, as well as a synchronized sexual harmony. If you want to take the relationship beyond basic attraction, though, you need to take time to get to know each other rather than just giving in to your more animalistic natures and focusing solely on sex.

Not Flowing Right: Mars is known as the god of war for good reason, especially on the home front. Its dark qualities are angry, arrogant, and proud, which can mean an explosive, even abusive, union in which one party erodes the other's confidence. It may lead to ignoring each other's limits and going way too far when tempers rise, causing one or both of you to forget what you initially liked about your paramour.

✧ Does this union satisfy you? If so, how?

✧ Are you or your significant other prone to anger?

✧ If yes, examine the reasons why.

✧ Is this a purely physical attraction?

✧ If this union is more than just physical, what do you want from it?

✧ Do you wish to build something longer-lasting?

✧ List the traits you like about the other person.

✧ If you are experiencing Mars's connections flowing well, then carry on, warrior.

Jupiter: "Altruistic Love"

A Jupiter connection is one of the most fortuitous two people can have, perhaps because it has the potential to bring out the best in both partners so you each can provide unselfish support and encouragement along the uncertain path of life. Jupiter expands anything it contacts, for better and for worse, so it also can magnetize one or both of your social consciences or worldly egos.

Flowing Right: You feel supported and growing, with increased confidence and shared beliefs. If you're in opposition on any subject, you could expand the wisdom and knowledge of the other or open their mind.

Not Flowing Right: You may become extravagant, encouraging the other to go over the top in their pursuits, which can lead to overindulgence or even danger, and emphasize their most harmful traits. It also can trigger arrogance and self-righteous or ignorant beliefs and behavior.

✧ Being a source of encouragement or inspiration is a marvelous feeling. Keep this in mind, and note when your ego is expanding so you can keep it in check.

✧ Can you think of unions that encouraged you positively?

✧ If you have time, check your charts to find a match to Jupiter.

✧ If you don't have time to fully check your charts for other matches, examine how this union helps boost your confidence or makes you feel supported.

✧ Have you experienced a union that made your ego (i.e., pride, ignorance, or anger) grow?

✧ If you are experiencing Jupiter's connections flowing well, then carry on as you are, oh enlightened one!

Saturn: "Serious Love"

A connection to your Saturn sign indicates a relationship in which both of you are willing to make a commitment and put in the work. Saturn is a glue that binds two people with a sense of security and responsibility for each other, with one or both of you maturing, learning, and growing.

Flowing Right: You appreciate the secure feeling of a mutual commitment. Respect is a big deal for both of you, and if it can be maintained, this relationship has the potential to last.

Not Flowing Right: This can be like leaving home to escape a rigid and restrictive parent only to repeat the dynamic with the first person you fall for. The glue may make you feel stuck.

✧ Try hard to allow your partner the freedom to grow and, if you have assumed or accepted a parental role as opposed to lover or partner, work to bring back the romance to the union. Have compassion and lighten up.

✧ Are you or your significant other prone to being too serious too soon?

✧ Do you feel restricted in your unions? If so, why do you think this is?

✧ Avoid blame that will block your progress at any cost. Write down a few examples of which unions you think have Saturn connections.

✧ What do you love about yourself when you are committed?

✧ If you are experiencing Saturn's connections flowing well, then carry on as you are, king/queen/gender-fluid monarch!

Uranus: "Rebellious Love"

A connection to Uranus often results in an electrifying relationship that awakens different aspects of both of you. For example, with Uranus in Scorpio, you'll find new insight when it comes to power or power struggles and sexuality; with Uranus in Aquarius, pay attention to humanity, the climate emergency, and higher causes. Think rebel *with* a cause.

Flowing Right: Your mind is open to change and productive revolution. Of course, that revolution simply may be how you see yourself or the world, or you may team up and become activists for a larger cause. This is an unpredictable connection, so there is unlikely to be a dull moment or a feeling of being settled. It jolts both your compassion toward each other and feelings of empathy toward humanity in general.

Not Flowing Right: This pairing can be disruptive, resulting in chaos, shocking revelations, and uncomfortable associations in the areas of your life associated with the sign it falls in. Uranus wants to enlighten you, and will do so forcefully if you ignore it, which can lead to years of excitement or to throwing in the towel and seeking something more stable instead.

Love Notes

✦ These connections are potentially life-changing but rarely comfortable. They can help you see the world through a different lens, which is imperative for soul growth.

✦ Be grateful to the person who is waking you up to their perspective, especially if you were previously fixed in your view of self and the world.

✦ Did or does this union open your heart and mind? Or evoke compassion?

✦ How?

✧ Do you wish to do more for humanity and the planet? If so, start small and try to be more compassionate toward yourself first and then roll it out to others.

✧ If you are experiencing Uranus connections flowing well, then Godspeed, courageous one!

Neptune: "Idealistic Love"

A connection to your Neptune sign often triggers the fairy-tale sort of romance you read about in novels or see in films. This relationship is sensitive, compassionate, and caring. This love feels inspirational, even written in the stars. Even better, it has the potential to last for life. (Think *The Notebook*.)

Flowing Right: Your relationship feels gentle, kind, and understanding. It is a meeting of creative souls, as artistic talent or a mutual love for the process, that attunes you both and results in living more creative and spiritual lives.

Not Flowing Right: This sometimes-idealistic love means that neither can see any faults or flaws in the other, even when they are potentially harmful. Or maybe it's a tendency to escape from what both see as harsh reality that triggers an unhealthy codependency with alcohol or drug misuse at its heart.

⬧ Have you ever experienced a love that felt predestined?

⬧ If yes, what was the attraction?

⬧ What does creativity mean for you?

⬧ Have you ever loved a creative soul other than your own?

⬧ Describe that relationship.

⬧ Are you spiritual? What does that mean for you?

⬧ Is your partner spiritual? Describe their why or why not.

⬧ If you are experiencing Neptune's connections flowing well, then carry on inspiring artists and poets with your beautiful love.

Pluto: "Intense Love"

A connection to your Pluto sign ensures total transformation. Pluto associations are empowering and life-changing, and the sexual chemistry often simmers.

Flowing Right: This connection can be liberating, but rarely is it calm. Intense feelings and buried pain or emotions from past unions are likely to be triggered so both of you can transform for the better—if you respond with honesty and not defensiveness.

Not Flowing Right: If you're not comfortable with the intensity of this growth, this partnership can be destructive, or even abusive. If left unchecked, expect many battles for supremacy.

⬥ This union requires patience and persistence. If both are willing to put in the work, incredible rewards are possible.

⬥ Check your motivation behind your words and actions at all times, especially when times get rocky, and gently encourage your partner to do the same.

⬥ Do consider the other person's feelings when you express yourself?

⬥ Is this intensity something you enjoy? If yes, ask yourself why.

⬥ If you are facing manipulative behavior, review why you attract, or enact, this. It's time to go.

⬥ If you are experiencing Pluto's connections flowing well, then carry on as you are, oh powerful one.

Chiron: "Healing Love"

*He showed me his scars, and in return he let me
pretend that I had none.*
—Madeline Miller, *Circe*

A connection to your Chiron sign often results in a healing union that helps one person, if not both, grow emotionally and spiritually. Chiron is known as the teacher and healer for good reason, because both play a pivotal role here.

Flowing Right: This connection brings the potential to move on from past wounds with a feeling of security and trust that is quickly established. Expect your own healing and teaching abilities to emerge.

Not Flowing Right: If you're not careful, old wounds are triggered, insecurities take root, and one or both of you sees your self-esteem diminished.

✧ Do you think you have healed emotionally from past hurts?

✧ If not, ask yourself how long you will allow this pain to control you.

✧ It's time to free yourself. How can you do this? What's one step forward you can take today?

✧ Does your partner or love interest have similar wounds?

✧ Does this attract you? How is this beneficial?

✧ Make a vow, right now, not to react to new people and situations based on old wounds.

✧ How does that feel?

✧ Keep trying. Soon enough new habits will form.

✧ If you are experiencing Chiron's connections flowing well, then carry on as you are, oh healing one!

North Node of the Moon: "Destined Connections"

A connection to your North Node often feels like you have met before; there's a sense of destiny and fate. It may even mean that you help each other grow on a soul level and progress toward enlightenment.

Flowing Right: The passion is clear, as is a resolve to establish a strong and committed relationship. Working toward a common goal or aspiration is also likely, whether you are friends, colleagues, or lovers.

Not Flowing Right: One or both of you may feel like the

other "owes" you something, or takes the relationship for granted, expecting the other to stick around come what may.

✧ You feel as if you have found your soul mate, and that may be true; however, it's important to help each other grow with love and to retain healthy boundaries.

✧ Do you both feel that this is a soul mate union?

✧ What does that mean for you?

✧ Do you ever feel as if you take each other for granted? Or feel taken advantage of?

✧ If yes, then stop, because life is fragile and impermanent and you don't have time for that. Nurture yourself and your relationship.

✧ If you are experiencing North Node's connections flowing well, then carry on as you are, soul mates!

South Node of the Moon: "Past-Life Associations"

A connection to your South Node feels like you have known the person forever. This particular bond indicates (by sign) where you have been in a past life, or even in your early life, by revealing past character traits and interests.

Flowing Right: The immediate sense of comfort feels like you have known your partner for years, even if it's only been moments. You may be able to work through a previous karmic issue you had with them or a similar situation, which will help you see how far you have come. The other person can act as a mirror from days gone by.

Not Flowing Right: You may feel yourself sinking back to old habits and revisiting the past, which is only a good thing if the past habits were good, too. Your past-life connection may not have been a fruitful one, so take your time to get to know your partner in *this* incarnation.

Love Notes

✧ This person may have been star-sent to help you grow or to see how much you already have grown and achieved. Or you may be the teacher who can help the other leave behind harmful habits and learn to love themselves.

✧ When you met, did you feel as if you already knew the person?

✧ Do they remind you of helpful or harmful past habits?

✧ Ask yourself if this union is healthy. Be honest.

✧ If not, speak up without blame and express your fear of destroying the progress you have made.

✧ If you are experiencing South Node of the Moon's connections flowing well, you've grown from past mistakes, so keep learning and expanding!

The Love Realms

In this section, I touch on the different categories of love, or the love realms, but focus primarily on how each of the twelve signs operates within every realm and their compatibility with the other signs. You learn all about the love realms and find out which one speaks to you the most. Then you discover how to match the signs with your own chart or that of your friend/lover/love interest (so be sure to find your ascendant/Moon/Venus/Mars sign, too). I also offer tips that help you transform passionate love into enduring love—or *reaching nirvana*, as I call it—which is the soul mate connection that transcends one lifetime and continues into the next.

Whether you want to analyze your current union or are embarking on a new relationship, it's useful to define the realm in which you are operating. Some begin with the fire of passion, which can result in total combustion or transform into an earthed and enduring love. Some begin with affectionate or compassionate love, which may become passionate. How the relationship begins doesn't determine where it will end up, but recognizing the love realms is crucial and will enable you to monitor your own behavior, track your progress, and adjust when necessary.

Passionate Love
This Falls Under the Fire Signs: Aries/Leo/Sagittarius

There are so many different styles of love, but perhaps the one most accountable for our complete loss of sanity is the fierce and furious passionate love, also known as erotica, from Eros, the Greek god of passion and fertility.

Passionate love creates unparalleled desire and the kind of euphoric highs people chase with drugs or exercise. When it's based on lust, sexual desire, overindulgence, or obsession, what begins as a whirlwind can escalate into a tsunami. It also inevitably causes devastating lows if either person becomes ungrounded in their behavior or unrealistic with their expectations.

Love unions often start out this way, and when viewed with clarity, handled with a sense of perspective, and equally respected and nurtured, they can result in enduring love.

◇ Take a fresh perspective: What if this love is another soul's compassionate way of teaching you something about yourself?

◇ Think about a time when you felt or witnessed passionate love. Most of us remember a standout experience.

◇ How did it begin? Was it purely physical or aesthetic?

◇ Did it fizzle out? And if so, why do you think this was?

◇ How do you feel when you think about it now?

Enduring Love
This Falls Under the Earth Signs: Taurus/Virgo/Capricorn
There is no magic formula that leads to enduring love. It takes work, rooted in reality, pragmatism, and, of course, love. Passionate love only lasts a few years at most, but what replaces it is far superior. This certainly doesn't mean the passion must die; it just

metamorphizes into something far more stable. Both parties must be real and honest enough to grow, and both are required to face themselves before understanding, compromise, and open dialogue is possible.

We have been fed romantic myths for so long, and I believe your dreamboat is out there waiting for you, if that's what you want. But here's the thing: each of us has our own kingdom of the heart and mind, which needs to be stable and respected, and we should come to each other's aid, but the kingdoms don't ever become *one*. To wait for another person to complete you implies that you are not already whole. That wound will inevitably attract another wounded person.

No one can give you what your own heart and soul is willing and, indeed, contracted to give. To attract the right one, you must first become the right one. The good news is that you can retain your own power and still surrender to real love.

Enduring love is achieved when both parties feel a sense of peace. This is true happiness, as opposed to chasing pleasure, which is often exciting but rarely tranquil.

✧ What does enduring love mean to you?

✧ What do you imagine are its benefits?

✧ Note how many times you use the pronouns *me, my,* or *I* in your responses and how many times you factored in your (potential) partner.

✧ What qualities do you have or require in your partner?

✧ What do you think the winning ingredients would be in the union?

✧ Which of the winning ingredients you want do you possess? List them.

✧ Which of the above do you believe are challenges, and how many can you say you have or do already?

✧ Do you perceive security and status as a priority?

✧ Bookmark this page so you can refer to this section a bit later when we discuss solutions to common issues in love.

Detached Love

This Falls Under the Air Signs: Gemini/Libra/Aquarius

Nonattachment is a form of love we mortals find rather challenging to grasp, with *grasp* the operative word. We cling to our preconceived notions of how a union should, or will, be based on our expectations of what another person could bring to our lives. It often has very little to do with reality, and air signs deal in reality as a commodity. If a person loves from a detached perspective, it can be infuriating for some signs and liberating for others. These people rarely just free-fall (except for Libra, who is often in love with the very concept of love—and concepts are not easy to actualize).

Those who practice nonattachment encourage us to review our basic understanding of love and what it means to us. It's not to be mistaken for manipulative or controlling behavior, and there are no mind games behind it. Instead, it is one of the highest forms of love one person can offer another. It isn't based on the primal "I love what you can do for me" or "I love how you make me feel." It's more like, "I will love you without strings" (which is not the same as "without respect"). It begins with friendship and respect and rarely ends in just one lifetime.

Detached love is also the most misunderstood version of love, which leads to many unions failing when they needn't have. When we think of detachment, we wrongly assume it means "indifference," which isn't the same thing at all. We may feel that someone doesn't love us enough to display attachment or assert ownership, but it is, in fact, often the contrary; detachment can be the highest form of respect. Air signs working within their flow are the least possessive of all the signs. They value independence and freedom, which doesn't equate to being unfaithful; it just means they don't like to feel trapped by someone else's concept of how they ought to be or how the union should appear to the outside world.

We may look on in wonder as air signs form friendships with their ex-lovers' husbands or wives, happily spending holidays with their former paramours. To them, it makes absolute sense, and everything about their way of loving has to make sense. Air signs believe that once you have loved someone, you always love them, and that friendship lasts for lifetimes. Air signs "gone right" let their partner be who they are and allow them to grow into who they want to be without placing demands on them. When it works well, it's incredible.

Some of the other signs struggle with this form of affection, perceiving their lover to be cold, and if they lack maturity or have insecurities, they will attempt to push their air sign's buttons with displays of jealousy and other harmful emotions (which usually leave their partners looking to hit the eject button). There is little point attempting to play mind games because air rules the mind—it would be like a child attempting to beat a seasoned chess champion with primary school moves.

✧ Have you ever experienced detached love? If so, after reading this, has your understanding changed in any way?

✧ Have you ever offered detached love?

✧ How do your expectations match the union you are in, or those you have had?

✧ Think about the difference between nonattachment and indifference.

Nourishing Love
This Falls Under the Water Signs: Cancer/Scorpio/Pisces

Love is one of our basic requirements, and our parents provide us with our first experience of love, for both good and bad.

We each began life in our mother's womb, during which—and in the months and years that followed—we must have experienced some level of nourishing love or else we wouldn't have survived long enough to be reading this. Some Eastern cultures teach that a baby removes all the negativity from their mother during the process of childbirth to express their gratitude for housing them and giving them precious life. Ancient scriptures say we will never be able to repay the karmic debt we owe to our parents so, no matter our relationship, we need to detach from any weightier emotions and show respect. Knowing what this kind of detached respect looks like enables us to form balanced partnerships. If we have issues with Mother, it negatively impacts the relationships we have with women (and ourselves, if we are female), and the same can be said of any issues we may have with Father. We must work through any parental issues honestly and then release them.

When my clients are embarking on a new love journey, I encourage them to heal their own wounds first. I suggest that they observe both their own and the other person's relationship with and attitude toward their parents. That was their first experience of love.

Letting go of unrealistic expectations or previous hurts, so we are freed from the prison of the past to enjoy the present and plan for a brighter future, is key. Life is too short to allow past disappointments to ruin the present, and if we're always looking backward, we miss the magical experiences offered along the way.

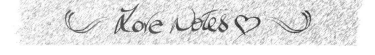

✧ How is your relationship with your mother?

✧ Think about how this impacts your relationships with other women and, if you are female, your expectations and opinions of yourself.

✧ Do the same for your relationship with your father.

✧ The above are our first experiences of love and form a foundation for all the others. Do you have any unresolved discord with your parents that you need to forgive, accept, and leave behind?

✧ If so, write them a letter and then burn it (safely), releasing any resentments.

✧ Forgiveness is your key to releasing the past and living a rewarding present and a love-filled future.

Love is a universal energy, but we must go beyond our preconceived ideas of its losses and gains. We need to nourish both our hearts and others', which in turn helps heal humanity—and the collective "we" needs it because we have managed to get into a hot mess due to a lack of love for ourselves and Mother Earth. A person who is loved glows, and they share that glow with others. When you love from your heart, it's liberating. When you give your partner total freedom and they bestow the same gift upon you, neither of you will ever feel the need to restrict or control the other.

In many traditions, it is widely accepted that a person can die of a broken heart. (Here in the West, on the other hand, it's diagnosed as depression and we are often prescribed drugs to numb the pain.) We lose ourselves to broken hearts when we become too attached to our expectations, which creates a tendency to cling to a perception of what we thought we had or could have had. True love is liberating, not restrictive, and we must give each other room to evolve.

We then have a choice: we can heal and learn by looking into our own behavior, without blame and judgment, or we can close our hearts and vow never to love again.

◇ If you have suffered a broken heart, how much of it was due to your own attachment (i.e., your expectations for what *could* or *should* be rather than what was)?

◇ Were your expectations based in reality?

◇ Did you see or feel red flags? If so, what were they?

◇ What did you learn? And how much responsibility do you accept?

◇ How could you handle things differently the next time?

◇ Start now by releasing blame and forgiving those you feel have hurt you.

Self-Love
Governed by the Sun

Self-love needs to be practiced every day. It enables us to gently assert and set boundaries, which leads to healthy relationships. Self-love is the practice that gives us the confidence to trust ourselves and our decisions, which means we live well and pursue our interests and goals with confidence and unselfishness. It also gives us room to grow with compassion for self, which rolls into our relationships and, indeed, into all we do.

Self-love often gets confused with ego, vanity, and selfishness, but they're not the same. Self-love is not about buying new clothes, finding the best filter for your selfie, or getting a massage. It's about trusting your innate self-wisdom.

This is easier said than done, but it's worth the effort. A lack of self-love can lead to unbalanced unions with an aversion to intimacy or connection, neediness and insecurity, or a desperation for another's affection. Generally, this kind of baggage is too much for someone else to take on in the long term. When you love yourself, this self-respect plays a key role in how and whom you love: you avoid giving your heart, the very thing that keeps you alive, to someone who cannot take care of it.

When we understand that birth, life, and death is a process, and how we experience the present is a matter of personal choice, then we can move on from the past and embrace a new reality. *This* is self-love, the key ingredient in happiness, come what may, and the superior path toward our own liberation.

Compassionate (Selfless) Love
Governed by Neptune

Selfless love is never self-serving; it works to foster an environment of care, attention, and respect, rather than seeking personal gain through a relationship. This stable relationship can develop into a passionate soul mate union that transcends one lifetime.

Compassionate love is detached (not indifferent) and keeps the other person's well-being and happiness at the forefront. We often feel it for strangers in trouble or those who are suffering. As we saw daily during the coronavirus pandemic, doctors and nurses risked and even gave their lives without knowing their patients or expecting anything in return, and they continue to do so every time they show up to work. This is selfless, or compassionate, love.

Opening Our Hearts

We all show our love in different ways. The signs and our birth charts play a big part in figuring out how to go about mastering the art of love—and it is an art. All forms of art require inner discipline and commitment to the process. Not only that, art and love go hand in hand. When we put our whole hearts into anything, it can leave us vulnerable. No other emotion has inspired so many works of creative expression, which is why musicians, poets, and other artists are often emotional about their work—they dedicate themselves to their art completely. Love requires the same kind of devotion and self-discipline.

Love is often packaged as a commodity—a product or an asset to market, buy, sell, and discard when it no longer serves our needs. But buying into this brand of "love" is not the road to liberation. Instead, it locks our minds and imprisons our hearts. Love is not cheap. It can't be purchased off the shelf. When we comprehend the value of real love and recognize it when it's offered, we will surge in the right direction, toward radical openness. We won't feel afraid of expressing our needs or communicating our true feelings.

Some say being too open makes us vulnerable and weak. It's true that openness derives from the soul, and we ought not to bare our soul too soon, not until we know who, and what, we are dealing with. But if we take the time to get to know someone and nurture each other and the relationship with patience and understanding, allowing ourselves to be seen is a form of beautiful vulnerability. If someone rejects us for revealing ourselves, we ought to thank them and move on to finding our true soul mate. It can be hard to intuit the right time to open ourselves. For this we need to trust our instincts. Many of us are *unearthed* and out of sync with the land, however, which makes us insecure, puts us out of balance with our true natures, and stifles the inner wisdom and confidence necessary for making smart decisions. When we are not secure within ourselves or our relationships, we cling to the notion of others making us whole. Only our connection to self, to the earth, and to the universe will award us with that wholeness, in this life and the next.

In love, the surrender required means we open and become vulnerable by dropping our mask. Ultimately, know that you are a child of the universe, sibling to the stars and the moon. This life is impermanent and one of many, so relax into yourself, ease into a union, and try to have faith in the gentle whispering of your soul.

The kind of love we feel also depends on the relationship we have with another. We love our parents and family in a way that usually falls into the category of affectionate love, which is governed by the Moon.

Unconditional love, which is also influenced by the nurturing Moon and responsible Saturn, is usually first experienced with our family and, especially, our children. Yet Buddhism advises that each person on Earth has been our mother at some point in our many lives so we should try to extend that sort of love to all sentient beings. The real goal is to work on our ability to love without expectation. Anything less causes us suffering. When you only want the very best for someone, even if that means they leave you behind, and even if it's painful, then you are working with the high vibration of unconditional love.

How the Signs Love

If you don't yet know your birth chart, read through the following elements and make a note of the traits of each that speak to you strongly. You can bet that if you do read your whole chart, the traits you've noted will feature prominently.

The Fire Signs
Aries/Leo/Sagittarius

Fire signs are learning about loyalty and perseverance. They love in an all-consuming way similar to passionate love. They are not overly cautious and throw themselves headfirst into any union in their quest for excitement and stimulation. When you are involved with a fire sign, it can be hard to breathe or imagine your life before they entered it. Often, without being conscious of it, they expect loyalty and devotion but don't know what that looks like.

By the time maturity sets in, and it will at some stage in this life or the next, they develop a more stable attitude without losing that flame that warms both partners.

Not Flowing Well: Fire signs can become addicted to the chase and drama of high-octane love and selfish in their pursuits. When they feel that they have won, they may lose interest. They can be so caught up in getting their needs met, they trample over their lover in the process. Unless they have strong earth or water elements in their charts, or learn to view their union as needing care and attention, they run the risk of failing to achieve anything enduring.

Flowing Well: When working with their flow, fire signs are incredible. They love with gusto, and if they are loved equally in return, they make their partners the center of their universe so everything and everyone else revolves around them. They are exciting and unpredictable, which can be a joy in an often-humdrum world. If they have decided to build a successful union, they work hard at it, adding sparks if they feel that the passion needs reigniting.

That energy and fire make their partners feel alive in ways no other sign can quite muster.

The Earth Signs
Taurus/Virgo/Capricorn

Earth signs are learning about impermanence and spirituality. They need to balance a natural tendency to seek status and power above all else. Many are looking for security in a world where, really, there is none to be found. Impermanence is a tough reality to fathom, but as soon as they realize happiness and peace come before money and gain, they can settle into magical unions. That said, they take relationships as seriously as they take everything else, and they often make wonderful partners. Before making commitments, earth signs, in their flow, take time to analyze the pros and cons, rarely jumping headfirst into anything. You know when they have done their due diligence because when they say they are all in, it's for the long run. When they finally make promises, they do all they can to keep their word.

Not Flowing Well: Often driven by worldly pursuits, earth signs judge people and situations harshly and may forget about the joy love can bring. In fact, they may unconsciously deem joy to be a tad frivolous. If someone matches their expectations of how a marriage or relationship should be, they will commit, but this is a one-dimensional way to perceive love. By the time they've analyzed the scenario, their lovers have marked them as aloof, demanding, or just plain difficult and have long since left—probably for a fire sign who brings the passion or an air sign who can turn spontaneity into an art form.

Flowing Well: A pragmatic and grounded earth sign brings a sense of security to their loved ones, who know their hearts are in safe hands.

Earth signs appreciate small gestures and happily support their partner's wilder schemes or endeavors. One word of warning: any flirtations with their friends will turn them cold and sour, so don't even go there. Public image and respect mean everything to them, so knowing this will keep you in good stead in the long term.

Those who work strongly with their earth often like to be with lovers with opposite qualities, but their morals and integrity have to be in alignment to make the match stick.

The Air Signs
Gemini/Libra/Aquarius

Air signs usually believe that if you truly love someone, you always will love them. Because friendship comes first, that love lasts for lifetimes.

Air signs love from a detached perspective. They let their partner be who they are and allow them to grow into who they want to be without placing demands on them to fulfill their own vision or ambition. Still, their lovers may perceive them to be cold and push their buttons with wild displays of emotion or mind games. Needless to say, no one will be happy in this dynamic.

Not Flowing Well: Like some fire signs, air signs need to work on their attitude to commitment. They may view attempts at intimacy as manipulation or a ruse to trap them. They can be quick to bore, high maintenance, and promiscuous (aside from Libras, who are usually more willing to stick around). Air signs work well with multifaceted partners who gently challenge them and help them *want* to commit. When they finally make that promise, they learn and grow, both personally and as a couple.

Flowing Well: Air signs are predisposed to cerebral connections and intellectual stimulation. They fall in love with a person's acumen, their bright mind, and their ability to provoke thought and spark debate. They enjoy nothing more than a friendly verbal sparring match and a lover who will bend their mind with profundity, not profanity. They need space but also stimulation, attention, and open communication to resolve misunderstandings or other issues.

Falling in love with a person's mind is a sure bet on an eternal bond. Unlike everything else, the mind never dies; it continues to form future lives.

The Water Signs
Cancer/Scorpio/Pisces

Water signs believe love is worthy of commitment. When they fall, all that joy (and pain) will last them several lifetimes. They generally require a formal commitment and emotional security and see marriage as a sanctity that will save them from loneliness and bring them stability.

Even within a long-term relationship, they don't often speak of their emotions; they expect their partner to automatically know what's going on. Scorpios in particular communicate via intuition and feelings and expect everyone else to do the same. Feelings are their love language, so take care of them. Unless they have lots of fire or air in their charts, they are usually the first to settle into a partnership and stop looking elsewhere.

Not Flowing Well: Water signs have such high expectations, it can be hard to meet them. There always seems to be something that "just doesn't feel right." Because of that, they can remain stuck in the past and hold grudges like no other sign, not realizing we are solely responsible for our own happiness, for better or for worse, and no one else is to blame when things go awry.

Water signs can be defensive and prone to overreacting if they are insecure, when they are tired, or if someone pushes their buttons. All water signs change moods on a regular basis. Try to avoid taking it personally, or you will be in for a rocky ride. Shrug it off, and soon enough, a smile will spread over their face as they sheepishly reach out to hold you and make amends. Don't expect a "sorry" or a meaningful conversation, though. They expect you to know it had nothing to do with you personally and they didn't mean it.

Flowing Well: Water signs are among the best caretakers of their partners and families. If they have a sense of humor, and most do, their playfulness and sense of fun are second to none. They appreciate the small gestures, so your efforts won't go unnoticed.

They can be shy at first, which is intriguing to most other signs, but then allow you in to the gentle, creative, and loving beings they are.

Love Signs—Constellations

You've probably guessed why Scorpio is also known as a scorpion, but have you ever wondered why Capricorn is a goat or Virgo is a virgin? Before you embark on the upcoming Part 2, "The Signs Combined," let's take a look at how the twelve constellations got their names. All are depicted as people or animals, except Libra, the scales.

Aries

Aries is depicted as the ram because the ancient Greeks believed that the constellation looked like a ram's head.

In Greek mythology, Aries, the winged ram with the golden fleece, was called upon by Nephele to save her son from his father, the king, who was told he needed to sacrifice his firstborn child to prevent a famine.

Taurus

Taurus is Latin for "bull," and although it was named by Ptolemy only in the second century CE, it's one of the oldest documented constellations, with cave drawing references that date back to the early Bronze Age.

Initially created to mark the position of the sun during the spring equinox, Taurus is most associated with agriculture and the birth of spring.

In ancient mythology, Zeus was believed to have transformed into a handsome white bull to seduce Princess Europa. It worked: they had three sons together and, in a show of gratitude, Zeus awarded the bull a place in the night sky as a star for all eternity.

Gemini

Gemini is Latin for "twins," and the mythology behind this constellation dates back to Babylonian times, when the stars Castor and Pollux, the great twins, were thought to have been gods.

In Greek mythology, the two were said to have been half brothers, and when Castor, the mortal, was killed, his devastated demigod brother asked their father, Zeus, to immortalize them together in the heavens.

Cancer

When Ptolemy discovered the Cancer constellation, he decided it looked like a crab, which is *cancer* in Latin.

In mythology, the great crab was sent by Hera to defeat Heracles during his twelve labors. Some say Heracles booted the crab into the heavens, where it became a star. Others say he killed it with his club, so Hera awarded it a place in the night sky as a show of gratitude for its colossal sacrifice.

Leo

Leo is Latin for "lion" and was named after the Nemean lion that was sent by Hera to defeat Heracles during the twelve labors, although there are a few different versions of this myth.

The Egyptians worshipped the lion as a god because the constellation's appearance heralded the summertime, when lions bathing in the Nile would coincide with flooding, which nourished the crops.

Virgo

Virgo is the Latin word for "virgin." There are a few versions of the mythology, so I will share the one that resonates most for me.

Virgo is believed to be Astraea, the goddess of innocence and purity, tasked with holding the balance of the earth and its seasons steady. Astraea opened a box and unwittingly released envy, hate, and jealousy into the world but managed to close it quickly, before hope escaped.

Libra

Libra is Latin for the "weighing scales," a symbol of deliberation.

Libra is associated with Themis, the Greek goddess of divine law and balance. When she and her daughter Astraea (who became the constellation Virgo) left Earth and took their places in the heavens, Themis took the scales of balance with her, which is now the constellation Libra.

Scorpio

Scorpio is named after the constellation Scorpius.

In Greek mythology, Orion was the son of Poseidon, god of the seas, and was said to have been the most handsome man who ever lived. He and the goddess Artemis requested of Gaia that she create a huge scorpion for them to weaponize. The scorpion consequently stung and killed Orion.

Sagittarius

Sagittarius is Latin for "archer" and was named by the Babylonians after the god Nergal. It was originally depicted with wings, two heads, and a scorpion stinger in its tail.

Later, when the Greeks adopted the star, Sagittarius was named after the mythological centaur, depicted drawing his bow, with the arrow aimed directly at Scorpio's heart in case the latter misbehaved.

Capricorn

Capricornus translates to "sea goat" in Latin.

In ancient mythology, Pricus was the immortal sea goat who desperately tried to prevent his children from seeking land and becoming the frolicking four-legged goats we know today. Pricus was devasted at the prospect of facing eternity alone after they went to land and begged Chronos (Saturn) to let him live out his immortality in the skies, from where he could see his children, no matter how high up on the mountains they grazed. Hence the constellation Capricorn.

Aquarius

Aquarius comes from the Latin word for "cup" or "water bearer," which is confusing because it's an air sign.

In mythology, Zeus coveted Troy's most handsome prince, Ganymede, so he transformed himself into an eagle and stole away Ganymede in his talons, forcing him to act as both servant and lover. Ganymede rebelled, and when he was expected to serve Zeus the cup filled with ambrosia, magical water, and wine, he tipped it out onto the earth, causing floods and chaos. After his initial fury, Zeus was impressed by Ganymede's courage and awarded him a place in the heavens as the star Aquarius, also known as the "wave maker."

Pisces

Pisces is depicted as two fish swimming both away from and toward fantasy and reality.

In the Greek tale, Aphrodite and her son Eros transformed into fish to escape the monster Typhon. In a show of gratitude, Aphrodite awarded the fish a place in the heavens.

2

The
Signs
Combined

When you look up into the night sky, to that busy celestial metropolis, remember that some of the starlight we now see was emitted up to two and half million years ago. Similarly, the emotional situations and intimate relationships we are experiencing have their roots firmly in the past. These karmic effects of our actions and inactions many lifetimes ago are what lead to "instant" recognitions with relative strangers and feelings of déjà vu.

We may meet one of our soul mates and stay together for life. This is a sacred union between souls that evolves over time and elicits the courage to trust and conquer insecurity and fear. A true sacred soul union is free of our tendency to weigh down others with heavy expectations. It offers us space and freedom to explore the universe and grow. But not all unions are meant to last. Perhaps we meet again to change the way we treated someone in the past— relationships are an opportunity to forgive and progress. If someone treats us badly, acceptance is not always love, but we can thank them for the lesson and then graciously detach so they can't do it again. Perhaps we then raise our standards to evolve and meet our twin flame, the one who ignites the light we already have within.

This is one life. There have been many before, and there will be so many more after, so think about how you can change the game *now* for the present and the future. It's in your hands.

How to Combine the Signs

Read on to match your star signs with friends, family, and lovers. However, please note that these pairings also will ring true for other astrological connections you may have when you study both of your natal charts. For example, if you are Gemini Sun sign with the Moon in Aquarius and your partner or friend is Aquarius, in addition to reading Gemini–Aquarius, you could read Aquarius–Aquarius, too.

As you read, take note whenever something rings true and pay attention to any forceful reactions because they surely will lead to interesting nuggets. Even more, if something you read irks you, explore what's happening. Growth, in its truest form, begins as annoyance. As my teacher once said, "The critic is our guru."

Now, let's have some fun.

Fire Signs Combined
Aries–Aries
RULED BY MARS

Picture lighting a stick of dynamite and waiting for the explosion. It may take some time for the wick to burn down, but that blast is coming. The Aries–Aries combination is always feisty and can be marvelous because both tend to move on quickly and let go of grudges. It's so refreshing after being with other lovers who constantly regurgitated old issues or told you that you're *too* this or that. In this union, both partners are too much, full stop, and neither is likely to criticize the other for it because that would be like scolding their own reflection—and an Aries is known to love their reflection. It's important to exercise self-love, too, because if you don't, you are likely to attract an Aries lover who loves themselves enough for both of you.

Your Aries twin most likely will stick around after the explosion, in stark contrast to prior lovers. They just didn't get it! Your Aries both gets it and will help clear away the smoldering debris. They might even pipe up with something supportive, such as, "Well, we needed a new carpet after all," or "This actually looks like a scorched piece of art now—I like it!"

SHARED TRAITS
This thrill-seeking, adventure-loving, passionate, and impatient duo may set the party on fire or unexpectedly leap from a plane, dragging

you with them. There is rarely any in-between—unless one partner had early life encounters that dimmed their natural dynamism or poured water on their ego. If that is the case, then that passion simmers somewhere below, always ready to surface as aggression, passive-aggression, fury, or an out-and-out temper tantrum.

These two usually make for an honest union; they are often so thrilled to have found a kindred spirit that they delight in making their partner happy. They have finally chanced upon someone who will stay up late on a school night and face the consequences later, a lover who won't ever bore them or chastise them for their extravagance (the gifts flow freely, if generosity is in their nature), and this bodes well.

This union has the potential to be raw and authentic, leading to soul growth and the ability to stand the test of time. Watch out for imbalances if one has a more furious temper, which needs to be discussed openly, addressed, and worked through. Try using the child's "time-out" approach or sending them on a 10K cross-country run with a really heavy backpack.

REACHING NIRVANA

If you are both working with self-awareness and in your flow, you're able to drop the masks of societal conformity and be yourselves, which can feel like coming home after a long time of scaring off lovers and suppressing the very dynamism that makes you irresistible. Gentle communication is key, as is allowing your partner to be independent yet stating calmly when certain behaviors are hurtful.

With the planet Mars as your ruler, you can get worked up quickly, and before you know it, you're breathing fire and wondering why everything is burning. Outwardly or inwardly, you get angry, which makes it tough to sustain a long and happy union. Anger is not an attractive trait. It is destructive for you, never mind anyone else, and can lead to all sorts of health issues, so this is something you can work on—together.

If you are an Aries who loves another Aries, contemplate the following:

✧ How often do you relax together or gently communicate?

✧ When either of you feels angry, how do you handle this?

✧ Work on your patience, which doesn't mean simply putting a lid on anger. Anger is the gun, and the triggers are other emotions such as fear or pain.

✧ Instead, when blood begins to boil, examine the root cause, which is always linked to your own reactions.

Aries–Leo
RULED BY MARS AND THE SUN

These fire signs are not known for their love of peace and calm, but it's exactly what they need to make it work.

Aries is known as the ram and Leo as the lion (or lioness). If a Leo has an unbridled rage, they may devour their ram and then regret it. But if they meet their match—and this union has all the ingredients necessary—it can be heaven on earth.

It is wise for a Leo never to forget that an Aries is born of Mars, the god of war, and if anyone dares to take them on when in their full fiery flow, they usually come out for the worse. An Aries rarely admits defeat—they may lose a battle but are better equipped than most for a full-on war and just keep going—and a Leo is a sore loser.

Only a Leo (or a Leo ascendant/Moon/Mars) will, and frequently does, take on the ram. If they are noble beasts who prefer to quietly assert their sovereignty, that's all for the better. But if they're the cowardly type of lions who skulk off to lick their wounds or rally support for their war elsewhere, it's for the worse.

MUTUAL ADMIRATION

When this union is working well, it's marvelous for both, as long as they can learn when each needs to take their turn showing their mutual admiration.

An Aries loves to win at any cost, and this plays out at work, with their family, and certainly with their lovers, but if it's too easy, they get bored and move on—or subconsciously make their significant other want to move on.

A Leo, on the other hand, secretly believes that they are far superior to all other mere mortals—until, that is, they meet an Aries. Slowly and surely, they develop an admiration for their partner's drive and strength, which are qualities they also possess, or want to. This is when the angels sing and harps play inside their huge hearts.

A Leo is generous with their affection and adoration, when—and this is a *BIG* when—they feel emotionally and physically indulged. But an Aries is not prone to indulging or pampering anyone. In the initial stages, they usually can settle their differences physically, either in the bedroom, on a racetrack, or via another competitive setting. When the sparks calm down, though, an Aries will feel outraged if they are always the one to acquiesce or tickle the lion's tummy and tell them how fabulous they are. It bores them to have a needy partner or one who requires attention on demand—nobody can demand anything from the child of a god! This indulgent behavior will only be tolerated by an Aries if the lion is wise, as many are. An Aries appreciates smart and sincere guidance and advice, and a Leo loves to give it. If an Aries perceives that the advice comes from a loving place, they will stop and not only listen, but also be open to hearing.

If, on the other hand, the Leo steps onto the stage and begins to brag about how right they always are or what happened when a past love failed to adhere, or they try to manipulate an Aries into doing or acting how they want, or their arrogance kicks in, either all hell will break loose or the Aries will head for the door.

An Aries requires inspiration from their significant other. They like to be excited and kept on their toes but also must be sure of their loyalty. A Leo desires loyalty but won't give it freely unless it is first given, which can lead to a dizzying merry-go-round.

An Aries also needs mental stimulation and can be tactless to save time, which they highly value. Their tendency to be domineering can wound the pride of a Leo, who becomes indignant when a lesser being tries to tell them what to do. But here is the thing: an Aries in its flow is one of the only zodiac signs that a Leo will respect enough to do what is asked, as long as it's not asked too often.

An Aries is commanding and usually for good reason, but if either partner has failed to do any self-improvement or introspective work on themselves, a titanic clash between two of the zodiac's biggest egos will ensue.

REACHING NIRVANA

An Aries is enchanted by a Leo's warmth and strength, for when they love, they do so wholeheartedly. For this reason, an Aries will gladly make moves to soothe their partner's insecurities. In return, a Leo sees through an Aries's brave facade into the inner workings of their heart and mind. This gives them an extraordinary ability to understand each other, and they can create their own world in which they relish the friendly rivalry and enjoy the finer things in life without being judged for their extravagant tastes.

The Aries is poised to benefit from the advice, warmth, love, comfort, and understanding on tap, which is exactly how the Leo likes it. In turn, the Leo admires the courage, dynamism, and excitement provided by their ram, which dissipates the likelihood of an intergalactic fight, turning the union into an unrivaled love.

If you are an Aries who loves a Leo, contemplate the following:

✧ Are you gentle with your lion's insecurities? Do they annoy you? If so, ask yourself why.

✧ Do you see through their prideful behavior?

✧ Do you feel that you give more than you receive? If so, can you discuss compromise with loving-kindness?

If you are a Leo who loves an Aries, contemplate the following:

✦ Do you tell your lover what to do or try to boss them around? If yes, ask yourself why.

✦ Do you give wise advice? If so, do you brag about it afterward? If yes, why? Are positive results not enough? Please know that this is a major turn-off for Aries (and everyone else).

✦ Do you take more than you give? If yes, please address this and try harder.

✦ When your heart is generous and open, you bask in your own sunlight, so try this in every given moment, without attachment to receiving something in return from the other person.

Aries–Sagittarius
RULED BY MARS AND JUPITER

If both parties enjoy high-octane fun, verbal sparring matches, and global adventures, this partnership will brim with inspiration and give both a mechanism to balance their fire with earth and air.

Now, a fire-on-fire union can result in mega-explosions, too, as each struggles to get their individual needs met. An Aries may lash out, reacting defensively and swiftly, but a Sagittarius almost always can win an argument with their red-hot-poker tongue and unbeatable aim of the archer they are associated with. An Aries is secretly left in awe by the often blunt and tactless delivery of that truth—unless it's aimed at them, in which case an argument may erupt. In fact, an Aries loves to be argumentative for the sake of a good debate or just plain sport. While in their flow they value the truth, but they rarely enjoy having to face their shortcomings or flaws. Their ego will fight those truths to the death.

A Sagittarius is rarely malicious (unless they have afflicted planets in neighboring sign Scorpio). They are playful, with a kind heart, and quick to check themselves. After (always *after*), they will apologize if they hurt someone in the name of truth—but by then it may be too late because an Aries can hold a grudge for as long as a Taurus or a Scorpio (well, almost), and they have exasperatingly long memories. So although the battle may seemingly be lost, as they are left red-faced by their truth-slaying lover, be careful that they have not declared war, silently adding to their to-do list to get you back—which they undoubtedly will.

FLIRTATIONS

Both partners tend to be night owls. They can effortlessly mix work and extracurricular socializing and will resist going to bed in case they miss a single moment. They love to mingle and be stimulated by novel experiences. This is where tensions may arise.

A Sagittarius, if working with the masculine element of the sign, can be extravagant and flirtatious and, like an opposite sign Gemini, walk a fine line when it comes to fidelity. For them, if an affair is not physical, or if it's purely physical but not emotional, and so forth, it's fine. In other words, if they are not all in, as in mentally, spiritually, and physically, they have done nothing wrong. Of course, we all know that's not the case, unless both parties are okay with it, and an Aries (if in love) is *really* not. There are all sorts of ways to be unfaithful without getting naked—even flirting with someone else, however innocently, can be hurtful. An Aries needs to feel and, more importantly, be seen as their lover's number one. This can lead to discord because a Sagittarius needs to feel free and will state indignantly that they were "just being friendly" or "helpful." Even if an Aries may not be able to put their finger on what exactly triggered their upset, it has led to insecurity and outrage. The archer must be mindful to not gaslight their ram, to have empathy, and to look at their own behavior. For an Aries, the outrage often stems more from being publicly disrespected than plain old jealousy. Although they will fight for their love for a certain amount of time, if the debate on what constitutes infidelity continues, it will leave them cold, and eventually they will leave.

REACHING NIRVANA

Both signs need a common goal and will defend the underdog in the face of adversity and criticism. A Sagittarius is usually more outspoken and active in that respect because they have an innate need for fairness and justice for all. An Aries takes a little more time to step off the self-serving conveyor belt, but when they do, together the two are a power couple personified and make remarkable strides toward the betterment of society.

If you are an Aries who loves a Sagittarius, contemplate the following:

✧ How did your partnership begin? What was the attraction?

✧ If either of your needs have changed, have you openly discussed this?

✧ Have you been honest throughout the relationship? If not, be honest now and write down what you really want.

✧ If yes, and your needs are being met, recognize your tendency to be a tad self-serving and ask yourself if you are you doing all you can to meet your partner's mental, spiritual, emotional, and physical needs.

✧ If not, make a list of small changes you are able to make. Bookmark this section to check back in with yourself, or ask your partner if they've noticed.

If you are a Sagittarius who loves an Aries, contemplate the following:

✧ Do you press your partner's buttons to cause a reaction or gain attention?

✧ Are you happy with a monogamous union?

✧ If yes, is your partner? Have you discussed this?

✧ If no, repeat the exercise. If you are not both on the same page, be prepared to let each other go. You cannot change another person or deceive them. It's awful karma in the long run.

Leo–Leo
RULED BY THE SUN

These lions light up any room with their presence, making even the dullest experience sparkle with potential. The warmth of their glow is so irresistible, it's easy to see why they are ruled by the Sun. They bring vibrant energy and solar power to everything they do. There are the insecure types of big cats who seek attention, recognition, fame, and gain and then there are the attractive, quieter, powerfully confident, and noble beasts who always get what they want. Either way, they command respect and devotion. When this loyalty is deemed sincere, they stick with each other and let down their guards in ways that only blue-blooded monarchs can do. They need to feel proud of their lover, and when they do, they encourage and support each other's loftiest dreams.

They often prove to be incredibly compatible, devastating any prior lovers or present hopefuls who fade into insignificance after they couple up. Strong, proud, and often fearless, this is a cosmic pairing.

INDEPENDENCE

If you know anything about cats, you'll know they value freedom above all else. But that does not mean they want the freedom to roam around with other lovers. On the contrary, a Leo elicits trust and demands fealty and consistency.

When Leos combine, they often feel that they have the world

at their feet, and unless they have contradictory, or afflicted, Moon signs, they usually do. Together they hold court, but when they fight, everyone needs to step back. This is usually part of their foreplay, and rarely do they make it public. Working in their flow, they are reserved and private beings and soon escape from partners who wound their massive pride or take their issues outside the home. If you look past the arrogance or false sense of pride, you'll experience an unrivaled generosity of spirit and a heart bigger than any you have ever encountered. That heart vibe coupled is as magnetic as the poles.

REACHING NIRVANA
This match usually works best when one party exerts more masculine energy and the other veers toward feline femininity. This is because both are highly competitive, either secretly or overtly, yet strangely, they also like to know their place. The former likes to protect, defend, and provide, expecting the latter to worship them with unyielding love and affection. Both quietly compete for superiority, which certainly keeps the sparks flying.

As with all fire combinations, patience and freedom from anger is vital so both partners feel heard and the union may flourish.

If you are a Leo who loves another Leo, contemplate the following:

✧ Are you able to lead and take a back seat equally?

✧ Would you say you enhance each other's virtues? Vices? Or both?

✧ Does your lover enhance your innate qualities, such as courage, strength, and generosity?

Leo–Sagittarius
RULED BY THE SUN AND JUPITER

In its flow, this is a bright, lively union, with both fire signs possessing an enthusiasm for life and a sense of play that makes those flames dance for everyone else to watch—much to the delight of the Leo, who basks in the attention.

At best, Leos are noble, discerning, and just. They've usually worked hard for status or recognition and persevere to become the best at what they do, even if they've had to overcome many challenges to get there. That's why they rarely will commit if their partner doesn't have a story the Leo perceives to be "worthy."

A Sagittarius, meanwhile, is honest and wise. Often they have had to overcome ignorance or bigotry and will look at any lover they see as less than worthy as a mere fling.

Both have a strength of character that either needs to be matched or, at the very least, complemented.

LUST AND THEN LOVE

When these two have gone through the initial lust stage and are entertaining the possibility of love, the result is a bond that wasn't possible with any prior lover.

A Sagittarius is a prophet, a philosopher, and an optimist (unless they have been worn down by a Leo or have challenging aspects in their full natal charts), traits that a Leo finds so charming and admirable, they forget to compete or take a superior stance, which is rare.

They are both independent, but when they commit and come together, their mutual strength is a force to be reckoned with, especially if they take up a noble cause. Both signs are masculine, which can work well because shared interests and the practicalities of life are often a driving force, and buried emotions and resentments are few and far between.

This union creates sparks that can last many lifetimes—or result in both continually vying to be top dog, which becomes exhausting, until one usually gives in to keep the peace. That's unlikely to be a prideful Leo; if they're operating in a low vibration, they are rarely keen to look at their own flaws and, like a Taurus and a Scorpio, may resort to a bitter sort of blame. Meanwhile, a Sagittarius lives by the law of fairness, so always being the one to compromise won't work for long. In short, unless they both know they need to grow, or are willing to learn how and, more importantly, when to cooperate, this partnership is filled with misunderstandings and battles of ego that can erode the self-esteem of both.

REACHING NIRVANA

That being said, no two are better equipped to help each other grow, even if it's uncomfortable. They fall in love hard, which makes them *want* to make it work. The archer never stops delighting in shooting arrows of truth, aimed at taming their lion's ego. (Of course, too much will make a Leo retreat to the jungle to lick their wounds.) On the other side, the lion is relentless in their wish to refine and advise their brilliant archer, but equally admires their faith, honesty, self-effacing humor, and integrity.

If the Leo's bossiness becomes too much to bear, the archer will take a hike—but secretly, they dig their lover's wisdom and take more notice of it than they admit. They just can't tell the Leo how much they support them for fear of advancing that unstoppable ego.

There is unlikely to ever be a dull moment. With honesty (at which a Sagittarius excels, even if tact is lacking) and sincerity, both can help each other see how marvelous life is when ego is curtailed and real love wins.

If you are a Leo who loves a Sagittarius, contemplate the following:

✦ Are you bossy? If so, can you temper this?

✦ Do you show off? If no, fab. If yes, why do you need to?

✦ Do you always have to win? If so, ask yourself why.

✦ Do you praise your archer's qualities? If so, super! If not, why?

If you are a Sagittarius who loves a Leo, contemplate the following:

✦ Do you tease your lion? If so, do you check your timing?

✧ Is your Leo wise? If yes, tell them; if they crow, explain how this impacts you.

✧ Do you communicate with love and without anger?

Sagittarius–Sagittarius
RULED BY JUPITER

When these two combine, it can be mutually refreshing because both are on some sort of mission to bring truth to the fore and expose corruption. They cannot believe they have survived this long walking the lonely path of righteousness by themselves, and this is where it gets interesting: depending on what element their Moon signs are in, they can be pompous and far too blunt but will try, and keep trying, to clear the air when misunderstandings arise. And they will. Spectacularly.

If one of them has an earth sign Moon, they are likely to be the more pragmatic; if one has a water sign Moon, they are governed more by emotion and are likely to offer a gentle sensitivity. Both are on the relentless pursuit of knowledge and have an optimistic outlook, which means they excel in learning; the more they discover, the happier they are. If one or both nourishes the other's mind with soulful information, this union is set to last. Working in their flow, they encourage each other to study and grow, both academically and spiritually.

Because growth is a major factor in keeping this union alive, ignorance is not usually tolerated for long, and they are the first to fact-check the other's claims and relish poking holes where they can, often publicly. The archers are easygoing, love to laugh and banter, and are game for teasing—unless they have strong water in their full charts, which makes them overly defensive or prideful.

The problem with seeing their significant other as an extension of themselves is that nobody can live up to such high expectations or journey along an ego trip long-term. Jupiter, the "judge," rules them both, so they can be slow to empathize and lightning fast to slam down the gavel, rarely seeing beyond black and white into the multiverse of color, which is also known as other peoples' truth.

FORGIVING

These two are magnanimous people who live in the present, which makes it easy to move on from discourse, disagreements, and even betrayals. If the partnership fritters out, they rarely become enemies; they prefer to choose to remember the good times and the qualities that initially attracted them. They rationalize quickly and compartmentalize issues that would send other signs into therapy. However, if they have Scorpio or Virgo planets close to their Sun signs, then the opposite can be true.

They are both clever and kind-hearted and can quickly get down to the cause of someone else's bad behavior, which dissipates tension or bad blood. They also make exceptional friends, although they are not so hot on consistency, so one or the other usually keeps abreast of any scheduled commitments or dates.

REACHING NIRVANA

Sagittarius is ruled by Jupiter, the planet that magnifies any sign or planet it conjoins with. Because of this, when these archers team up, the potential to exacerbate their vices is enormous. If one previously gambled for pennies, then combined they will bet the house when playing a friendly game of cards.

Learning moderation is key. That said, this magnification also offers the opportunity to grow and support each other in overcoming unhelpful habits. Uneducated archers are ignorant beyond belief; there is no excuse in this age of free information to remain in this state, so researching their "facts" is a must.

Finding a positive common interest or hobby is a smart idea, but aligning with a higher spiritual vision will bond them in this life and for many more.

If you are a Sagittarius who loves another Sagittarius, contemplate the following:

✧ Does your partnership encourage you both to reach for the stars?

✧ Do you know when to slow down and stop? Is this something you can do together?

✧ Is either of you overindulgent? Can you monitor this?

✧ Do you check your facts?

✧ Are you both risk-takers? If yes, is this to your benefit? Or to your detriment?

✧ If the latter is true, talk to your lover and make a pact to address this.

Water Signs Combined

Cancer–Cancer

RULED BY THE MOON

These lunar babies are kind, gentle, and patient and never fail to show up for each other. Cancer couples understand each other's defensiveness and mood swings, as well as their need for comfort, which is why they are so well matched. They thrive together overall because both seek to build a solid future with each other and create a "perfect life." When they are self-aware enough to know that perfection can't ever exist in the future (it resides in any given moment, and that's all we have), this union can be magical, inviting friends and family into their welcoming home.

This relationship avoids much of the chaos and anxiety other zodiacal pairings may attract, so these two are monogamous for life. The only issue is that they may trade growth or excitement for safety, thus skipping the passionate phase altogether.

Cancers have a long memory for betrayal and trauma, in particular from childhood, which often haunts them. Even if they had a stable upbringing, no mortal parents could have given them enough of the constant love, affection, and emotional support they required to state that it was "happy." This makes them critical of folks outside the two of them, but rarely of each other. They give to the other the only thing that each has ever wanted: appreciation.

The other signs, especially breezy air signs, help them lighten up and laugh at themselves but eventually lose patience with the Cancer's tendency to stay locked in the past. Another Cancer, though, listens over and over, providing comfort as needed, and that's why most stay under the protection of their lover's shell when they eventually venture out of their own.

If neither challenges the other to accept and move on, then one or both may play the victim just for the other's attention. Wallowing in the feeling that someone *finally* cares for them can be detrimental to the progression of the soul. Unless they help each other see their own flaws and learn to forgive others, this can turn into an unhealthy codependency that isolates anyone who challenges them or jolts them into the real world—a world where there are always two sides to a tale.

SECURITY BEGINS WITHIN

Cancer desires emotional and material security, even though the former can only come from within, and the latter is a fallacy. No one else can truly heal our insecurities, and you certainly can't take it with you. This drive makes Cancers successful in the world of business because they believe that the more money, status, and power they attain, the more secure they will feel. They support each other to build dynasties with like-minded people. They also have solid morals and will encourage each other to achieve, yet to be fair and just. Working together is a matter of course, in some shape or form, as they have an unspoken pact to achieve stability.

Most need an official commitment, such as marriage, and have a strong desire to procreate, making little ones in their own image. They are mostly excellent parents but can smother their offspring or struggle to let them go or grow independently.

If they don't have children of their own, it's likely that the home often will be filled with stray animals and friends in need. When called upon to help, these two are so sensitive to the plights of those less fortunate that many dedicate their life to service (but not their wealth—they will bury themselves in gold-filled tombs fit for ancient Egyptian royalty).

REACHING NIRVANA

This pair has the rare opportunity to form something sacred within which both may safely grow and mature. If they can laugh at themselves, they will soar. They need to realize that it is important to bravely accept the true nature of impermanence, that our souls have been here many times, and will return, and we must learn from our experiences to reach nirvana. If both Moon children can help each other overcome the tendency to blame everyone else for their problems and accept that their challenges are opportunities to forgive, they can become the sort of golden couple most of us could only ever dream of. When they both accept personal responsibility and work to purify their karma in this life, they likely will remain together for many lifetimes, bringing loving-kindness to everyone they encounter along the way.

If you are a Cancer who loves another Cancer, contemplate the following:

✦ Do you hold on to past hurts? If yes, how does that help you?

✦ Do you give without expectation? If so, list a few times when you have succeeded at this.

◇ Do you practice forgiveness? Try to see things from a different perspective.

◇ Do you enable your partner in the blame game? If so, why?

◇ Do you believe in karma and cause and effect? Try to study this; it'll help you progress.

Cancer–Scorpio
RULED BY THE MOON AND MARS/PLUTO

Cancer and Scorpio magnetize each other almost instantly, and that, as they say, is that. Nothing will ever be the same again. Intensity, emotion, and perhaps even fury draw these two hard-shelled, soft-core folk together in the deep seas of empathy and feeling.

The Scorpio is charmed by the Cancer's natural gift for intuition, and the Cancer is secretly thrilled by the probing mind of the scorpion. Both signs set out to seduce and possess the other. For the crab, their seductive prowess is an art form, cleverly disguised as sweetness, a cool reserve, and the tendency to disappear when the sheer power of the Scorpio becomes overwhelming. That's not to say that the crab is manipulative, although they certainly can be, but that's a trait most frequently seen in the Scorpio. Both are driven by a need for guarantees and, when they meet, they realize early on that they have what it takes to achieve it in each other's arms. Nothing in life comes with a true certainty, but these two will come closer than any others.

A Cancer is so sensitive to the emotions of others that every so often they need to retreat and regroup, infuriating the Scorpio, who secretly fears that time apart or silence will break the spell they have spent enormous energy casting. But the crab is immune to any kind of enchantment spell or emotional blackmail, and that is what makes life with them so very interesting. A Scorpio can't help but make moves to control the other by ascertaining what motivates them; that is, until they encounter the lunar child. Once a Scorpio has taken possession of another's heart, mind, and soul, ironically, they stop trusting them, which is why, when trust builds slowly and steadily between these two, they find themselves feeling more secure together than they ever were apart.

They understand each other, too. The crab won't let go of past hurts easily but is rarely vengeful, whereas the Scorpio believes they are somehow karma's agent star sent to get even. The crab finds it somewhat amusing that they, the sovereign of grudge-holding, needs to spend time compassionately teaching the Scorpio what they, too, must learn—the gentle art of forgiveness.

KNOW THYSELF

This duo spends far too much time piercing through people's psyches and analyzing their characters to find weak spots. The crab does this to protect themselves against any surprises. And the Scorpio? Well, it's just because they think they can. Rarely do they look at their own reflections, though, so when they finally meet a lover who seems to know them better than they know themselves, the attraction is palpable.

Both are money lovers—one to combat insecurity and the other for power—so this partnership works best when they have equal assets, similar ambitions, or complementary skills that will help them achieve worldly security together.

REACHING NIRVANA

These two run the risk of taking each other down into the depths of low vibrations and the underworld of darkness. To work well as a couple, they need to develop kindness, unconditional love, and empathy for the other, keeping their hearts open and working on their own ability to trust. They need to be honest, which is hard because they are both secretive and prone to paranoia or evening the score. The crab is prone to internal temper tantrums, and the scorpion directs their rage or jealousy toward revenge or covert control mechanisms, so opening up is the only way to achieve enduring love. They can grow together if they retain mutual respect, study the workings of the mind, and understand the laws of karma and cause and effect as a daily practice.

If you are a Cancer who loves a Scorpio, contemplate the following:

✧ Are you able to offer your love without the fear of rejection?

✧ Do you help your Scorpio lighten up and move on?

If you are a Scorpio who loves a Cancer, contemplate the following:

✧ Do you panic when your crab retreats? If so, why?

✧ Do you hold a grudge? If so, develop the courage to forgive.

✧ If fear were not an issue, how would you operate in this union?

Cancer–Pisces

RULED BY THE MOON AND JUPITER/NEPTUNE

This is an idealistic romance that has the potential to last, but only with plenty of tolerance and self-reflective work. A mutual appreciation for the arts, music, nature, and the beauty of the world can bind them together, but only if the Pisces is evolved enough to empathize with their crab's predisposition toward accumulating wealth and hoarding money. When they realize this behavior is born from insecurity and an intrinsic fear of ruin, they are able to help the crab grow and to experience life through a different, less grasping, and more aware lens. Unless the earth element is strong in the Pisces's full chart, this fish rarely has any interest in money just for the sake of having it, and some even perceive it as the root of all evil, preferring to live a nomadic and unworldly existence, at one with nature. They know they need money, but their sensitive souls rightly see how greed and selfishness is killing this beautiful planet so they dislike materialistic people or pastimes.

The crab is driven by their desires for comfort, home, and family. They wish to nest in a cozy home and surround themselves with expensive trappings. In return, the fish can seem uncommitted, unambitious, and irresponsible, and this causes misunderstandings: one prefers to surf the waves of life, unencumbered by mortgages or debt, and the other needs a large safety net and can trample over everyone else to create one. If the Cancer is evolved and money is no problem, or the Pisces has strong Cancer/

Capricorn or Virgo planets in their full charts, these issues will rarely surface.

HOW THEY THRIVE

The sensitive crab is enamored by the unflappable disposition of the Pisces, who stays cool unless their lover repeatedly nips them with their pincers or refuses to give them sorely needed alone time, in which case they run the risk of being devastated by a tidal wave of emotional destruction. That aside, if they are both emotionally mature and self-aware, they may thrive because Pisces are sympathetic, kind, and wise beyond words when it comes to reading between the lines or intuiting the emotional reactions behind their snappy crab's behavior. And in return, an intuitive crab will give the Pisces the space they need and the freedom to just be. The fish likes to live and let live, and for this pairing to work long term, the crab needs to learn when the invisible "Do Not Disturb" sign is up.

REACHING NIRVANA

If they can take the time to get to know each other and respect each other's emotional needs, this union can be blessed for eternity. They both love art, creativity, and peace, although the latter is more a Pisces thing. Creative living, spirituality, meditation, and mind-training is beneficial to both, as is living close to the ocean or a body of water. The Cancer is ruled by the Moon, which influences the tides, and the Pisces is ruled by Neptune, the planet also known as Poseidon, king of the seas, so water heals both their souls.

If they focus on common interests and what makes them both happy, then with enough compromise for each partner to feel satisfied, they can soothe each other in ways only water signs know how to.

If you are a Cancer who loves a Pisces, contemplate the following:

✧ Are you materialistic? If so, examine the reasons behind this.

✧ Do you give your lover space without taking it as a personal rebuff?

✧ What are your common interests? Shared traits?

✧ Do you take your lover's emotional needs into consideration?

If you are a Pisces who loves a Cancer, contemplate the following:

✧ Are you patient with your lover? And they you? If not, you need to try harder. List a few ways in which you can act to improve this.

✧ Do you know how to ask for space without losing your temper?

✧ Do you communicate openly?

✧ Study the rule of three (Ro3) on page xvii. This is especially effective with crabs.

Scorpio–Scorpio
RULED BY MARS AND PLUTO

Casual or *flighty* are words never associated with this combination, whose chemistry is palpable. Physical attraction or passionate love is usually how this union starts, and emotional understanding comes later.

Both are on a mission, consciously or subconsciously, to secure a soul mate union. A Scorpio never enters anything without meticulous calculation, and when they've set their sights on a goal or a person, they make impressive moves to secure it or them. When they deem a lover worthy of their undying love, they dive in, dragging their paramour with them, whether they like it or not. The part of the marriage ceremony that states "'til death do us part" must have been written by a Scorpio because death is something that fascinates them, as do rituals, the occult, and sex. (The French are, as a collective, very Scorpio. We call passionate kissing *French kissing*, and their word for *orgasm* translates to "little death.") When these two finally choose to surrender themselves to a mutual passion, it's as if they die together and go to a heaven of their own making.

The Scorpio is sometimes depicted as a snake. A growing snake sheds its skin up to four times a year, and the Scorpio is constantly evolving, transforming, and displaying the process of birth, death, and reincarnation. They've mastered the art of reinvention.

The Scorpio is the best game player in the zodiac, whether in business or pleasure, because their poker face tricks us into thinking they have the winning hand, even when they don't. They fool others into believing that they don't care when, in fact, it's quite the opposite. They care so intensely that it can alarm them and everyone else, except their Scorpio lover, who gets it and gets them. This is both satisfying and unnerving. Rarely outside of their own reflection have they encountered someone who sees them and is unafraid.

People are often wary of the might of Scorpio, unless they, too, were born under that sign and ruled by the planet Pluto, the god of the underworld, also known as Hades. When these two team up, it's not unusual for thunder to crash and lightning to strike because this power and potential union moves heaven and earth.

When you meet someone who operates in the same way you do, it's life-enhancing and transformative, for better and for worse. Yet how it finally plays out is up to them. It depends on their level of self-awareness and the inner strength necessary to avoid the destruction of their self-esteem or sanity. They eye each other up with both respect and caution, ever aware of the power and desires simmering beneath the other's mask of cool indifference.

HONESTY

For this union to work well, they need to be, or at least want to become, the evolved version of the Scorpio: empathetic, intuitive, and understanding with a rare inner knowing. They know why people behave in negative ways and can help them overcome challenges and transform.

But the unevolved snakes are suspicious, jealous, at times unfaithful, and prone to betrayal, using sex as a weapon, mind control as a hobby, and drink or drugs to escape from the intensity of being born under their star. They have the capacity to hurt each other like no other combination, which is why communication is the only way to build something stable and loving. The Scorpio drive to get even and seek revenge is real, and they are, along with the Cancer and the Taurus, the most unforgiving of signs. Watch Gracie Film's black comedy *War of the Roses* to see a typical Scorpio-versus-Scorpio dynamic.

However, when they *really* pair up, these two *will* forgive each other. They both know how hard it is to exist as perceptive beings in this superficial world, and if honesty and truth are on the breakfast table each morning or at dinner with fine (preferably French!) wine, they will talk, hear, and conquer any world they set their sights on. The level of commitment is unparalleled.

REACHING NIRVANA
Owning up to their mutual tendency to hide hurt and pain, redirecting it toward revenge and getting even, is the way to attain enduring love. Both are protective and secretive and often too proud to express their real feelings for fear of seeming weak or experiencing rejection.

Pluto, as their ruling planet, gives them and their thoughts the power to actualize anything, which is dangerous in the hands of ignorance. The karma of a Scorpio is fast and swift to return, like a boomerang, so using this talent as a force for good is the way to progress toward a rewarding relationship with themselves and everyone else. It's also how Scorpios can work toward the attainment of our soul's true goal: enlightenment.

If you are a Scorpio who loves another Scorpio, contemplate the following:

✧ Are you secretive? If so, why?

✧ If genuine respect is present, jealousy cannot arise. Contemplate this.

✧ Do you engage in power plays?

✧ Do you suffer from jealousy or competitiveness? If so, what other emotions trigger this?

✧ Do you believe in karma? If so, would you consider that your thoughts, words, and actions also have the power to create negative karma toward you?

Scorpio–Pisces

RULED BY MARS/PLUTO AND JUPITER/NEPTUNE

This enchanting relationship entices both water babies into a seemingly destined union. Their language of love is almost always hidden from the rest of the world, and many relationships begin as a secret affair that only they can understand. These two keep each other bewitched with an unspoken bond of empathy.

The fish and Scorpio are (unless they have Leo/Virgo/Gemini Moons or rising signs) private beings, which is why they appreciate the fact that they don't need words to communicate. This relationship is a telepathic connection that can make them feel as if they are soul mates.

But watch out: an unevolved Scorpio is prone to jealousy and possessiveness, which makes them weak-willed and fearful of their own authentic power. And an unevolved Pisces is slippery and controlling, seeking only to lure the best worldly catch into their net. This low-vibration power play won't last for long, though, because the scorpion will soon lash out with a destructive sting, perhaps in the guise of a betrayal or another form of deception. Then the fish will unhook, disappearing into the depths of the ocean.

MUTUAL EMPOWERMENT

There is no better escape artist than a Pisces, which leaves both partners to quietly mourn their losses from different universes forever because neither can forget the other or the feeling that they have lost their true love.

The evolved scorpion, meanwhile, knows that true power is limitless and can be accessed without disempowering any other living being to stay on top. They have faith in themselves, the universe, or whatever they perceive God to be, which makes them instantly attractive to the benevolent fish, who is absolute in their confidence that to serve and make others happy is the point of life. For this reason, when they team up, they have an extraordinary opportunity to help others and create a meaningful life outside of a materialistic existence.

REACHING NIRVANA

If the Scorpio can check their motivation and loosen the hook on their fish, and if the Pisces can be honest and avoid their habit of disappearing physically or emotionally for long enough to work through any misunderstandings, this pairing has potential. They have an innate ability to communicate without the need for harsh words (unless Virgo is prevalent in either of them), but they must work to keep that gift alive.

Drugs and alcohol don't usually mix well for this zodiac cocktail, so clean living leads to a more harmonious and productive life with the mutual aspiration, and ability, to be of use to humanity in some way.

If you are a Scorpio who loves a Pisces, contemplate the following:

✧ Do you allow yourself to let go?

✧ Does the easygoing nature of your fish delight you? If so, why not try following their lead?

✧ Do you need to release harmful patterns or habits? What is your plan?

If you are a Pisces who loves a Scorpio, contemplate the following:

✧ Do you love your partner for what they have, or for who they are?

✧ How do you envision your future together?

✧ Do you help them lighten up?

✧ What sacrifices have you, or will you, make for your lover?

Pisces–Pisces
RULED BY JUPITER AND NEPTUNE

When these gorgeous children of Neptune finally meet, it's as if they have come home after a long and lonely journey. When fate casts her graceful hand, time stops—which is exactly where the issues start. These two are artistic souls, highly sensitive, spiritually inclined, and perceptive; some would say psychic. Fish usually find a unique way of escaping the demands of a mundane daily life and the noise of the real world's *busyness.* This may be in a healthy way, such as artistic endeavors or spiritual practices like prayer, meditation, or a higher belief in a binding universal truth. They have an innate creativity; they may paint and make art, play music, or spend hours with their hands in soil, cultivating food and flowers that grow abundantly under their touch. Or they may find the whole "life" thing too much to handle and try to escape via drink, drugs, video games, or by following the lead of so-called gurus. They can be deceived easily, in many ways, in their pursuit of oneness with the universe.

When two Pisces combine, they double their capacity to raise each other to the high vibration of the heavens and stars above, or lower down into the addictive cycle of unhealthy escapism, and rarely can there be any in-between. If they have grounded planetary aspects like earth, Moon, or Mars in their full charts, this can be balanced out.

They are not the fighting types, unless they have fire as Moon signs or other strong placements. Instead, they choose to settle disagreements or give each other the cold shoulder for days. I'm not talking the brutal ghosting a Scorpio does; this is more like, "I am not even here. You cannot see me, nor I you." Pisces are often said to be slippery, which can be true if they have Gemini or Sagittarius as Moon signs, but for the most part, they are honest, at least with each other, and the only time they fail to tell the truth is to save the other from pain or hurt feelings, which would hurt them just as much.

SOUL UNION

The female fish, or those who veer more toward the feminine aspects of the sign, is usually gentle, artistic, imaginative, and overflowing with a grace and humility that is like manna from heaven for the male fish. He feels as if he has met his twin flame, and the levels of perceptiveness and power of telepathy that exist between both is a wonder.

The masculine Pisces (or those with plenty of yang vibes) often has had to deal with ego-led, aggressive partners in the past, so this serene and sympathetic union is a double blessing for both.

REACHING NIRVANA

If both water babies focus too much or too little on worldly accumulation, fear and anxiety will arise. A blend of faith with pragmatism is the answer to building a lasting love, based on mutual trust and confidence in the law of attraction. Taking refuge in a solid, spiritual vision will hold them steady enough to surf the waves of impermanence.

Addressing any harmful habits together will assist their souls' growth and, if they work on projects they love and hold fast to faith in the abundant nature of the universe, all will be well.

If you are a Pisces who loves another Pisces, contemplate the following:

✧ Do you honor each other's sensitive natures?

✧ Try practicing the law of gratitude every morning and gauge the results.

✧ Do you indulge in escapist behavior? If yes, how may you moderate this?

Earth Signs Combined
Taurus–Taurus
RULED BY VENUS AND CO-RULED BY GAIA

These two magnificent creatures are appropriately matched to build a future based on the highest vibrations of love, loyalty, and mutual respect, a future that has all the potential to be content, calm, and abundant. Wrapped in the comfort of abundance is just how the bulls like, and perhaps even need, life to be. They, like most earth signs, are willing to work hard, expending enough effort to ensure that their personal relationships and professional lives flourish, which is why it's a good match (unless they have other disagreeable signs or planets clashing in their natal charts, which can lead to an entirely different union with its own set of struggles). By communicating honestly, without mind games or the will to control the other, their love grows strong like the roots of a tree.

Evolved bulls long for space, to breathe clean air and not feel rushed into anything. Forcing them into doing anything is a futile ambition. The long-game moves they make will have factored in some sort of eventual space where they can connect with nature and perhaps even grow their own vegetables or herbs. Life is short, though, and too much future proofing and planning results in them missing the moments of perfection in the present.

ENDURANCE

The ideal scenario that will allow this union to endure is country life, or at least as much time away from screens, phones, and the constant bombardment of information as they can get. Unnatural concrete and the unrelenting radio waves, courtesy of modern life, pound into them. Most know they regularly need to flee the city, but the rest just feel drained, unmotivated, and irritable with no clue why. Bulls thrive with free-flowing water, green pastures, and rolling meadows close by.

Taurus is also the sign of talent, and if they don't feel that they have their own, they readily will support others to help them flourish. It's usually easier for them to make money through the arts, music, entertainment, or architecture fields than other people.

When this union works well, the two nourish each other in so many beautiful ways: with encouragement and kick-ass strategies for their worldly pursuits and goals, or with enough kindness and support to drive each other toward greatness.

This is also a highly sensual love match. The Taurus is all about the body; a tender touch does as much, if not more, for these bulls as sexual encounters.

If they are unevolved, one or both easily can be triggered into becoming impatient if they feel unfulfilled professionally or are weakened by jealousy, like their opposite sign Scorpio. But this green eye is different: it slowly builds to a boiling point of bitter resentment and then explodes, which feels strange to them because most are cool-headed pragmatists who believe that if someone has worked hard for their achievements, they deserve success and happiness. The Taurus is usually the one who bats down any opposition driven by the actions or words of the unwell (and jealousy really is an illness). With one swift swat or a smart word—or the best weapon they have in their armory, gentleness—they can transform these lower vibrations into all-encompassing love through sheer force of will.

They choose their battles, partners, and allies cautiously and won't expend precious time or energy on anyone or anything that threatens to drag them down.

If either get stuck in the materialistic kind of life that offers no substance or sustenance for them, they suffer more than most—usually physically or emotionally—and fights for supremacy occur.

REACHING NIRVANA

These tenderhearted romantics are ruled by Venus, the planet that imbues beauty, resourcefulness, and grace, and they possess the superpower of attracting whomever and whatever they desire (eventually, but bulls are tenacious). They invest patiently and carefully, always planning with the long term in mind. Multiply that by two, and you can only imagine the never-ending well of possibilities for this couple.

I, however, have another theory. I first heard this from one such bull, my late astrology teacher and friend Derek Hawkins, who we nicknamed Granddaddy Gnome. We concurred that the Taurus sign is in fact cogoverned by Gaia, or Mother Earth, and for years, I have watched this theory play out. If Gaia influences a Taurus, their surroundings impact them majorly, so natural, clean environments and lives are the way for them to blossom.

Staying fit is vital for us all, but for the bulls and their partners it's imperative because it reduces the aggression within and builds much-needed stamina. A Taurus also needs to open and tame their mind, through mind training, meditation, yoga, or qigong, lest they become fixed in their body. To thrive together as soul mates, they, like their zodiac friends Cancer and Aquarius, are best placed to build a rewarding life away from the chaos.

If you are a Taurus who loves another Taurus, contemplate the following:

✧ Note your mood when you're in front of screens for prolonged periods. Note the same when you are away and in nature.

✧ Do you stay fit? If not, adopt a new twelve-week regime and track your progress.

✧ If you suffer from envy, try exploring the triggers honestly and adopt an attitude of kindness and grace for yourself or others who display this. It's not going to be easy, but envy is a mind poison, and tackling it is imperative to your happiness and well-being.

Taurus–Virgo

RULED BY VENUS/GAIA AND MERCURY/CHIRON

These two earthy signs are naturally attracted to each other for many reasons. The kind-hearted Taurus sees through the cool and composed facade of their virgin and is endeared by what they discover—innocence, eternal youth, and a tendency to want to see only the very best in others and make everything better. They value them enough to look past their quirks, which often manifest as slight obsessions and an annoying need to know every single detail before they set sail on any adventure—which at times will annoy the hell out of the Taurus, who was trying to plan a surprise, and then the Virgo will complain that they don't have the right shoes on, or a delivery was coming, or that they had a deadline. Other folks would sulk and vow never to charter a boat for a surprise picnic again, but the Taurus lets it all blow over their wise head and zones out until the Virgo begins to smile. All is well again in the land of love, and that is exactly how to handle a Virgo.

A Virgo can be tough, critical, and hard to get to know. But the savvy bull knows that underneath that prickly exterior, and when in their flow, you will find the most kind and powerful healer of all, who only seeks perfection—hence the need to micromanage and sweat the small stuff, stuff that the bull has long since dismissed as unimportant. The Taurus usually stays quiet unless asked to comment, and then they will gently offer their sage advice to a receptive Virgo.

NITPICKING

A Virgo is prone to nitpicking until they drive themselves, or their bull, mad, and the latter is not a wise move on any mortal's part.

Bulls generally swat away this behavior as if it were a tiny fly on their mighty tail. A Virgo appreciates this refreshing, nonreactive approach, and the same can be said for the bull in terms of how a Virgo loves them. No other partner (aside from another bull perhaps) is willing to hold the fort while their bull builds on solid dreams that will benefit both of them and their family. A Virgo will stand beside their Taurus for as long as it takes because they believe without question in their bull's skills and talent.

Bulls are possessive. They can deny it as much as they like, but that's an astro fact!

Children are a source of delight for both, but unexpected additions are rare; these two make plans and then plow onward long after many others would've given up.

Bulls value loyalty, and a Virgo is loyal to a fault. That's not to say they won't throw it in their bull's face from time to time, which certainly destroys some of the magic . . . some, but not all.

REACHING NIRVANA

We all know that a Virgo's high standards can never be met, but telling them that is like revealing to a Sagittarius, the "seeker," that the truth they incessantly chase rests always within. Why spoil their journeying?

The bull needs to know they can depend on their virgin through thick and thin, and only then do they offer eternal love and loyalty.

But a relationship between these two has a much better chance of some longevity when they have a common cause—and it can't just be the kids (who eventually leave home), a bigger house, or anything else worldly. Igniting faith in a shared higher vision will rejuvenate them and their union. A genuine spiritual teacher will help guide them, or starting meditation or yoga together, or any other practice that aims to balance mind, body, and soul will be good for these two.

If you are a Taurus who loves a Virgo, contemplate the following:

✧ Do you see through their controlling ways to their heart of pure love?

✧ If you have any resentments, write down a list of them all and then burn the list. Resentments do not help your soul's growth.

✧ Don't stop surprising your Virgo; they secretly love it.

If you are a Virgo who loves a Taurus, contemplate the following:

✧ Do you ever remind your bull of the sacrifices you have made or continue to make for the union? If so, why? The karmic merit of a good deed diminishes if one boasts about it or lords it over another.

✧ Do you praise your Taurus when they show their love?

✧ Are you able to laugh, both at yourself and together?

✧ Are you critical? If yes, try reframing your words and opinions with pure love.

Taurus–Capricorn
RULED BY VENUS/GAIA AND SATURN

It isn't unusual to witness a mature bull and an old goat happily grazing side by side in rich, verdant pastures—pastures they likely co-own because these two won't relax until they are debt free and suitably wealthy in terms of worldly possessions.

Thinking that the goat is dull or the bull a bore is nothing short of astro prejudice. Bulls are among the most multitalented, creative beings on Earth; goats are brimming with brilliance, regardless of their day jobs; and both have an impeccably timed, dry sense of humor. Such droll perspective is imperative for this union to work well and for the long term. Without it, they run the risk of taking themselves, and life, far too seriously, which can, indeed, result in the goat and bull transforming into bores.

There are always exceptions to these rules, and they can become opinionated or just plain bigoted. When they double up, it can be a painful experience for anyone who must suffer them for long. If they have power, things can become downright dangerous. However, this would only ever apply if one or both of them failed to educate themselves and allowed fear of change to hamper their soul's growth. A Capricorn fears failure and may close their heart if they have been disappointed, and bulls, well, they become the kind of bitter that makes you wince upon the slightest taste.

As a duo, they have enough sass and smarts to reach dizzying heights of success and an abundance of wealth. In fact, money and status are important to them both, but they run the risk of losing sight of the magic of daily life if that is their only goal. The bull secretly fears poverty, and the Capricorn prefers to tone down the excesses, unless they have a fire sign Moon or ascendant or are just insecure.

When these two combine, they have more opportunity than most to create something that lasts, be that a life, an empire, or a legacy. Bulls thrive when they are committed to a union that is going somewhere, and when they know they can trust their partner, they happily share their love and affection, and half of everything they own, without question.

The goat likewise will go the extra mile for their love (unless they have a fire Moon or air planet in their charts coercing them into mischief). They are equally as faithful and reliable, treasuring the steadfast kind of partnership offered by their bull.

Goats are the more adventurous in the bedroom, but the bull delights in the pleasures of the flesh just as much. These two may have invented the word *epicurean*, as a taste for the finer things always plays out in some aspect of their lives. They may settle for a humble shelter, but be sure wine will be plentiful and the bed linen will be fine.

ROMANCE

As a couple, these two are surprisingly romantic, yet their gestures are thoughtful, loving, and private, not grandiose. Rarely do they open quickly and, although bulls are often hesitant to trust, when they do, they are all in. Bulls expect their smart Capricorn lover to remember the little things, and they better never forget important dates, moments, or gestures their bull has made to show affection. When bulls cook, they use the freshest ingredients they can forage, and if the goat is unappreciative, they will be faced with indignance and an extremely cold shoulder until they talk it out.

Goats must shake off the habit of assuming that everything has a price and that is how things are valued. Bulls will snort and comment, "But I gave you my time," which they rightly value above all else. In return, goats get what they most desire from this partner: respect. They are intelligent, discerning beings, not known to grow complacent (a trait usually reserved for a Leo or Gemini), which suits this pairing well. They rarely subscribe to otherworldly beliefs, but even they know, within their souls, that they have found the one person who perhaps destiny manifested for them, and the boundless compassion they have for each other is cosmically divined to last a lifetime.

REACHING NIRVANA

Patience and moderation are key, and for this reason, before they become fully devoted, there may be many stops and starts. If one or the other needs to grow, clear debts (worldly or karmic), or release themselves from a past relationship or marriage, the two will, somehow, find their way back to each other at a later stage.

They need to commit to building an honest partnership because casual or illicit affairs don't work for them. Neither is (openly) spiritually inclined (unless they also have Aquarius/Pisces/Scorpio planets in full charts), but what is spiritual anyway? More importantly, an authentic "spiritual" person treats the earth, and all life, with respect, which these two usually evolve toward, holding a reverence for nature. Doing to others as you would have them do unto you is their motto.

If you are a Taurus who loves a Capricorn, contemplate the following:

✧ Do you push your opinions, or will, upon your partner? If so, why?

✧ Do you respect your partner? If yes, continue. If no, you must realize that this is key to the success of this love match.

If you are a Capricorn who loves a Taurus, contemplate the following:

✧ Do you appreciate the small gestures your Taurus makes?

✧ Are you able to laugh together?

✧ Do you consider your bull's feelings?

Virgo–Virgo
RULED BY MERCURY AND CO-RULED BY CHIRON

The world of the Virgo was such a weary place, filled with misunderstandings, reasons to worry, and endless imperfections of lesser mortals—until they chanced upon one another, *chanced* being the nonoperative word here. This sign does not like to leave, or credit, anything to such random gambles.

Virgos combined and in their flow are marvelously optimistic and just a little profound, like Winnie-the-Pooh. They possess bright minds and a quick wit that is utterly irresistible to their fellow sign. This is also true for those couples with any Virgo planets in their full charts.

The virgin is the purest and most charming of signs and, when in their flow, they refuse to succumb to the lure of suspicion or paranoia, preferring to see the best in others, rising to serve selflessly with their natural talent for healing. There are no beings on Earth (except, possibly, Scorpio) who have the power to heal us all, sometimes as doctors and nurses, but always by way of the heartfelt words they speak and their capacity to lift the spirits of even the weariest of souls. This partnership likewise nourishes in indescribable ways. Virgins can be as extreme as Aquarians, and when in a union, well, you can magnify that effect by one hundred: from a Mother Teresa style of healing to a wound that only a sadist would inflict.

When they form a union, they finally feel as if someone understands them and sees through their veil right into their heart, which is as radiant as the sun at first light. Like a Libra, a Virgo has unachievable expectations in general and, therefore, can see flaws readily while missing what they do have. Two virgins can come pretty close to the perfection they seek—that is, until one of them leaves the toilet seat up, replaces a book in the wrong place on the shelf, or puts empty jars of jam back in the fridge without adding it to the shopping list. The fact that the rest of the house is either like a bombed-out city or a manicured lawn is inconsequential; if you have messed up their order, fix the mess quickly or make them laugh fast and hard. Failing that, you can expect to be punished.

It's exhausting being a virgin, which is why we must cut them some slack and do what their Virgo lover does naturally: love them unconditionally and pump plenty of our heart into theirs until they know it's safe to surrender to the power of love. It takes patience and perseverance to coax a Virgo into the warm embrace of a relationship, but when you do, it's a union worth its weight in gold . . . and then some.

Loyal, honest, and trustworthy to a fault, these guys don't gamble, but they will bet on each other and support each other, 'til death do they part.

Unless they have a competitive sign (Leo/Aries) or a jealous sign (Taurus/Scorpio) changing their flow, they are not the type to hold grudges for long, or to play games, or to make moves to control each other. Their trust is absolute and, courtesy of co-ruler Mercury, they can communicate and will work hard to clear up misunderstandings.

LETTING GO

The unevolved or unhappy Virgo can become bitter with suppressed resentments, and that's not ideal because they then can drag their loved ones into the mire of their cynicism.

When they are evolved, they are open, accepting, content, and pure, but the opposite is toxic. Letting go is a concept made personally for them. Trusting that the universe has a plan and having faith in the better intentions of human nature will help them attract that vibe, and tribe, many times over.

REACHING NIRVANA

If two virgins are self-aware enough to face their own flaws with a view to mastering them and adopt an attitude of progress, not the martyrdom or self-flagellations some of them veer toward, this has all the blessings of the universe.

They trust each other's motivations and wisdom and, together, they can work toward creating an enduring love match.

Most are highly intelligent, and mind-altering drugs or excess alcohol consumption, wrongly used to tame the internal chatter, can lead to anxiety and paranoia. Avoiding the former and moderate use of the latter is best. Taming that brilliant mind via regular sitting meditation is also helpful. (They will argue that running or working out is the same as meditation, but it's not, even though both are beneficial.) Sitting with the mind and training it to be less discursive is something these two can conquer together, and come what may, joy in the moment will arise.

If you are a Virgo who loves another Virgo, contemplate the following:

✧ Be the partner you want to have.

✧ Are you able to face your flaws and embrace your virtues?

✧ What does a relationship based on trust look like?

✧ Do you blame others for your problems?

✧ What is perfection to you?

Virgo–Capricorn
RULED BY MERCURY/CHIRON AND SATURN

When these wise and cautious signs combine, they sidestep the star-struck lovers stage altogether and walk gracefully into a union of instant commonality. Some may say it's a boring match, but the goat and virgin would counter that those outward displays of emotion are an uncouth and an unnecessary drain on their vital energies, and neither appreciates waste of any kind. But do you want to know the real reason for their disdain toward public displays of affection? They are both extremely private people (unless they have Gemini or Leo as a Moon or rising sign vying for attention or recognition), and their business is their business. So if a lover or friend is anything less than discreet, they will walk away without a backward glance.

Finding another soul who thinks like them in an attention-seeking world is like finding gold in a mine full of narcissism. They don't fall in love; they walk right into it with open eyes. When they commit, they do so with a view that it's going to be for life, or at least for many years, and often the union, for one or both, has a purpose other than just romantic love, be it status, security, to start a family, or to create a legacy.

If you can't see it, it rarely exists for them, but if one or the other presents proof of a universal consciousness or higher power, the other listens attentively. Virgos are known to blather on, but goats listen and think carefully before responding with intelligent questions (unless they have Sagittarius as a planet close by, which means they may dismiss such poppycock, or a Gemini sign, which means they will argue, debate, and tease just because it's fun).

INDUSTRIOUS

If they are working in their flow, the Virgo and Capricorn believe in hard work and will not respect a lazy lover or one who is frivolous with money, time, or resources.

A Capricorn plans a long-term vision and solid goals with a tenacity for placing the correct boundaries and structure to achieve them, and they only celebrate when they have reached those milestones.

A Virgo is hardworking by nature, and they love to serve. Many have the notion that they will give back, or donate time to charity when they have enough security, but they fail to note that giving back to humanity can be a moment-by-moment decision that doesn't require grandiose ideals. If they haven't realized that helping others makes them happy, they may become cranky and even self-obsessed, which can be a nightmare to live with.

Correct being the operative word for both signs, they will rarely move together without a stamp of officialdom, which is why affairs won't last long for either. They are prone to embarking on secret trysts only if they are already thinking of leaving a spouse. They both care too much what the outside world thinks of them. Virgins are not usually the type to stray unless they are driven by a Libran planet and then they do so with the safety net of a new partner to fall swiftly into.

REACHING NIRVANA

Lightening up and not taking themselves or life too seriously is a must for these two. This eliminates the risk of them becoming old before their time and unfairly disillusioned with each other, when really, they're feeling a disenchantment with life itself.

Not becoming complacent and finding ways to enjoy the little pleasures is a smart move, as is practicing the law of gratitude. These two thrive when they cultivate the spirit of generosity and pure unconditional love. Capricorns can be kind and patient, and virgins bloom under this spell of acceptance.

Capricorns become younger as they mature in years, and virgins possess an innocence that ensures they rarely grow old. When they embrace the warmth of togetherness and a youthful enchantment at life's potential, they stay together . . . forever.

If you are Virgo who loves a Capricorn, contemplate the following:

❖ Do you take life too seriously? If yes, can you sidestep the need to be in control and let go to the magic of each moment?

❖ Are you prone to cynicism? If so, can you try to embrace optimism without fear?

❖ If you suffer with anxiety, try to remain in the present and avoid overthinking the future.

If you are Capricorn who loves a Virgo, contemplate the following:

✧ Are you able to see through to the pureness of your lover's heart? Try, because it's there.

✧ Do you know how to relax together?

Capricorn–Capricorn
RULED BY SATURN

When Capricorns look in the mirror, they see the only reflection they've ever been able to trust—until the stars align and they meet each other, that is. But not on some faraway planet, dodging meteors like air signs to find each other. No, they meet with their well-shod feet (goats have a penchant for fine shoes) firmly on solid ground. They are not known to bet on anything other than a sure thing, which is why they take a long time to open up and trust another person. This process is accelerated, but never sidestepped, when they meet a fellow goat.

Lovers who create drama for them or take them away from their all-important career-climbing, responsibilities, or ordered life would've been left on the sidewalk long ago. Goats won't ghost you; they will retreat to gather their composure and thoughts and then return to tell you, in a chillingly cool and firm tone, that this (i.e., you) simply isn't working. Just like their opposite sign, Cancer, they are learning how to master emotions. The former is controlled *by* them, but the goat makes sure they are in control *of* them, unless they feel safe, and then, and only then, will they allow their enthusiasm or passion to emerge. This may make them seem cold, but it's not as simple as that. They are ruled by Saturn, which I call the "Queen," and, if you know anything about sovereigns, you will realize that showing emotion publicly feels like a sign of weakness, and weakness often equals demise. Ancient astrologers called Saturn "father time," and this also fits because Capricorns value their time as a commodity and are not likely to waste much of it on anyone who may make them deviate from their quest for world domination.

The goats as a duo make the best parents and partners because they hold similar aspirations and rarely enter into personal or professional agreements until they have executed due diligence and made provisions for every eventuality. As nongoats know, life is a series of curveballs, though, and they are likely to be saddled with rebellious Aquarian kids or maybe spontaneous rams to learn that. But you can rest assured that when a goat makes you a promise, they will walk over hot coals to ensure that they keep it. This is their own, quiet, heartwarming way of telling you that they love, respect, and cherish you. Just don't expect any wild displays of emotion—except in the boudoir, where they unleash everything they've kept bottled up, and that makes this union utterly delicious in private.

DEPENDABLE LOVE

Unless one of the Capricorns has a fire or an air rising sign or planet close to their Sun, they will be dependable once they're committed but will remain ever cautious and watchful should their lover fall off their impossibly high pedestal. The late astrologer Linda Goodman described goats perfectly: they are born serious, wise, and discriminating and then they defy the aging process entirely by becoming younger as they get older. For this reason, it's not unusual for goats to find their one true love later in life, when they have accepted the fact that life is never certain. When they comprehend that impermanence is the only constant, they stop taking themselves and the dance of love and life quite so seriously.

If they have yoked themselves to a marriage for the sake of status, which is very often the case, or burdened themselves with a huge mortgage that hangs like a millstone around their elegant neck, then they will find a way to escape (eventually), but only if they have paid all debts and made sure everyone else is going to be all right. They value their honor, reputation, and responsibilities above all.

REACHING NIRVANA

These two have the bonus of knowing how the other ticks, so they can speed up the usually lengthy due-diligence process.

Both need to contemplate the impermanence of existence, which will lead to embracing a lighter, more spiritual outlook. Finding the right path to the universal source of life will boost their faith, and this word, or notion, is one goats struggle with from day one of their earthly existence. Faith that a higher power exists helps them bond on a much more profound and exciting basis, which leads to a peace-filled and rewarding union and attitude in this life . . . and beyond.

If you are a Capricorn who loves another Capricorn, contemplate the following:

✧ Are you a forgiving partner?

✧ Are you able to accept what is? Or do you strive for more?

✧ Do you understand the law of karma and impermanence?

✧ Are you defensive if your partner becomes emotional? If so, try harder to be patient.

✧ Do you honor your own feelings?

Air Signs Combined
Gemini–Gemini
RULED BY MERCURY

Let's talk about the twins. There are two kinds, obviously. First are the quietly knowledgeable, pensive thinkers, as immortalized in bronze by Auguste Rodin. These ingenious messengers unwittingly act as the go-between for humans and the universe. And then there are the mercurial, wily, and at their worst, ignorant twins, the tricksters of the zodiac, who bend the truth depending on what they want or are selling.

As the most interchangeable beings in the zodiac cocktail, Gemini can change from the former to the latter in the blink of an eye. This is seldom an easy or relaxed union. Any Gemini who believes they are straightforward and uncomplicated is as confusing to themselves as they are to the rest of us. They are always on the move, if not physically, then certainly mentally, with a mind that enables a lover or friend to either momentarily experience their trip to the "light fantastic" or short circuit; rarely is there ever any in-between. If you really think you know a Gemini, think again—they rarely know themselves. An encounter with these mercurial beings can make you catch your breath in awe or run for the door for enough oxygen to start breathing again. Either way, it's intense.

Lovers without any strong Gemini planets in their charts are mesmerized because their twin manages to live a life that is nothing short of an acid trip. But for this union to last, they are going to need to be an air sign or at least have one planet in the sign of Gemini. When you multiply it all by two, or four (as twins), prepare to be dazzled and captivated but never bored; this energy can become exhausting for less airy, mentally dexterous folks. With another twin, they'll feel that they have come home. But for how long, one will never know. And if you happen to be the twin with more water or earth in your chart and innocently question the other, their multicolored feathers will become ruffled and they either will become defensive or flee the scene, thinking that asking "What time do you want to eat?" is a covert attempt to stifle their freedom.

It's hard to face yourself when you're always in transit. Both (and all four) of you must beware of the baroness of busy lives because time will run away with you, as much as you try to pretend that it is you who is the master of time. This is a fabulous union for fun but not easy for longevity, only sustaining the tests of time and reality if one or both have partaken in serious self-improvement work, *and* if both are able to dig deep for a whole heap of patience.

STIMULATION DOUBLED

If a twin is evolved enough, they will either have grown weary of superficial encounters or have an earth planet or rising sign prominently in their charts—or will pop Valium or do other drugs in an attempt to slow the rapid movements of their bodies and discursive minds. Even then, unless they are highly evolved, this will be only a short-term fix that leads to other issues later. The ultimate solution is to detoxify their lives and train their mind to be still and present.

Unevolved twins relish in gossip and anything else that lowers the vibe for long enough to prevent their biggest fears—reality, depth, or emotional intimacy—from surfacing. They indulge in anything or anyone that distracts them from the fact that time may be running out for them. But on a soul level, they do know, which is why a Gemini–Gemini union has all the makings of success. If they are prepared to face their fears together, they can become both wiser and stronger together.

Mental aptitude, dry wit, and humor are their superpowers, which are key to achieving an enduring love that will enable twins to take life seriously—but never too seriously.

The evolved twin is a totally different being, one who has mastered the art of sitting still and realized the benefits of serious contemplation. They do this through mind training and meditation and then they become the greatest thinkers and smartest doers on Earth. Their potential has no bounds, and they are perhaps one of the likeliest of all the signs to solve the complex riddles of life;

reach enlightenment; and save all beings from the cyclic suffering of life, aging, sickness, death, and rebirth. When they sit still for long enough, they have the power to see beyond the veil of superficiality, and when they combine, you can multiply this potential by four and then some. Until then, they are to be found darting through social groups, gathering stimulation, half-truths, and other delights. When they finally encounter someone like them, they slow down for just long enough to take note. You can see the stars forming above both their heads before one or the other runs off again to hunt for a new experience in their eternal quest for excitement. They may return to each other, or they may not. Either way, they are unlikely to forget the encounter.

REACHING NIRVANA

For this union to work long term, it is necessary that both parties want to settle down, which requires understanding, patience, and unconditional love. Because they require varied social interactions, insecurity is not ideal and flirtations can become an issue. If an open union is okay for both parties, then perhaps jealousy won't be a problem, but this generally works well for one twin and less so for the other. Open and honest communication is fundamental; otherwise, misunderstandings and mind games are likely to arise.

Again, mental training is a must. Physical exercise also will help them come down to earth and realize that all the stimulation they seek is already there.

If you are a Gemini who loves another Gemini, contemplate the following:

✧ Are you comfortable with silence?

✧ Do you listen to your quiet inner voice? Do you listen to your lover?

✧ Do you know how to relax without using brain-numbing substances?

✧ Do you know yourself? And if so, do you take the time to know your lover?

✧ Have you ever tried mind training? If yes, keep it up! If not, try it together, and track your progress after a few weeks.

Gemini–Libra
RULED BY MERCURY AND VENUS

When a beautiful Libra, child of Venus, full of grace and serenity, meets a beguiling Gemini, who is as smart as a whip, they make a charming duo who live happily ever after. Except it's not quite like that. It can feel like a fairy tale at first, and with enough honesty, patience, and compassion, it could last "forever," although a Libra lacks patience, and a Gemini—well, honesty and compassion are often lofty aspirations for most twins.

A Libra is known to be gifted or at least greatly interested in the arts and also fair of face, which goes for those folks with Libra

Moon, Mars, Venus, and rising signs, too. Even if they are not conventionally handsome, when they shine their light on the object of their affection, they have a captivating energy, attracting the good, the bad, and the ugly. A Libra is deceptively strong but without aggression, and they are also shrewd. They know what they want—or rather they think they do—and they are not above using their beauty, sweetness, and gentle charm to get it.

But they are not interested in a fawning fan as a partner and secretly love a challenge (unless they are more mature emotionally or in years, in which case they will contentedly settle for a partner who amplifies their serenity).

Both partners want the whole package, but if the Libra senses they are not getting it, or that their lover is losing interest, they will line up the next player in their game of romance as soon as the climate is right. The Gemini is much the same in that respect, but they just keep moving. If they decide to surrender their treasured freedom, it only will be to someone who has sass, intelligence, and charisma in abundance—like a Libra. But they may find a Libra a little too demanding. The Libran "need" to be in a partnership can lead them into all sorts of trouble as they jump from one person to the next or settle for something less than they deserve. The person they need most is themselves, and until they accept who they really are and realize that their truest life partner is their own soul, they run the risk of hopping from one tragedy to another or settling for someone who was only ever suitable for a brief affair.

The twin is often easy on the eyes as well, which, coupled with their brilliant mind and lightning-quick wit, gives them the ability to seduce almost as easily as the Libra can. But the unevolved twin is capricious, slippery, and maybe even dishonest, and that won't wash for long with a Libra. Most are rather conventional, and a respectable, "stand-up" partner is rarely something they will compromise on for long. Even if the twin is rolling with their uneducated and undesirable side, their contradictory nature means that they expect their partner to be better than they are and help them grow. In particular, if both have earthy Moons, it grounds the union into something stable and lovely.

SUPPORTIVE

These air signs are compatible in many ways, but without dialing into reality or working with any of the more grounded earth signs at play in their synastry charts, it's not always a union of longevity. The relationship can be smooth sailing, depending on their combined full charts, or they may find themselves regularly dashed against the rocks. Gemini is a mutable sign, changing its mind depending on with whom it's conversing and how powerful the sway of reason or temptation may be. They give their word and then forget the whole conversation, which infuriates the Libra because they take people at their word and are almost as literal as an Aquarius.

A Libra will take time to analyze every eventuality before coming to a decision, which is why they are often unjustly perceived to be indecisive, but that isn't always the case. They, like the scales depicted in the hands of their ruler Venus, can see both sides. They happily will make excuses for their Gemini lover, who is busy chasing a new idea, and defend them to their friends and family who believe the twin is untrustworthy or trying to wriggle away from commitment.

The Libra will support their twin's ever-changing plans and new career ideas, chiming in with hints about the pros and cons. In return, the Gemini will offer the Libra a glimpse of just how fascinating life is when you have faith in the universe.

If anyone tries to control a Gemini, they will rebel. They may snap back with harsh words, or they may just decide they can't be bothered. A Gemini is immune to mental, physical, or emotional games; they may indulge their lover because it's amusing to see another player use the moves they have long since mastered, and they may even learn some new skills, but for an intimate relationship, only open honesty will help this union stand the tests of a love match between two competent players.

The Libra believes they are looking for a lover who will adore them, make them a priority, and chase them to the ends of the earth when required. But when they have those starstruck, fawning bedfellows, they quickly lose interest because seduction for them is as easy as a Sunday morning—until they meet their peculiar twin, who refuses to submit and has multiple personalities so it's impossible for Libra to become complacent.

REACHING NIRVANA

A Libra requires balance and will make deft moves to readdress any aspects of their lives that are out of kilter. If they feel that everything is too lopsided, however, they will swiftly move on, leaving the Gemini shaken by the coldness of it all.

For this union to work, both must be ready to settle into a genuine partnership and be honest right from the start about what they are looking for or discuss openly when the goalposts need to be moved. Both must avoid mind games or manipulation of any kind and refrain from trying to change their partner to fit with their own agenda. These air signs need to listen to and *hear* each other. They must not be angered by the prospect of change, because it leads to growth. Shared interests are paramount; if they don't have any, it's wise to find some both can take part in.

A Libra longs to give themselves over to love, but that won't hold the twin's attention or affections for long, so building a life together and still retaining their individual lives is a smart move.

Self-improvement and awareness of self will help them reach the heights of happiness and an enduring love.

If you are a Gemini who loves a Libra, contemplate the following:

✧ Are you honest with your lover about what you want and what you feel you can offer?

✧ Do you plan on making a commitment? What does that look like to you?

✧ Does this align with your lover's needs?

✧ Do you know yourself?

✧ Try meditation at home with your lover, and practice grounding exercises.

If you are a Libra who loves a Gemini, contemplate the following:

✧ Are you content with your lover? Are you trying to change them?

✧ Does your union check your boxes? (I know you have boxes!) If yes, great. If no, try to amend and compromise without expecting your partner to change.

✧ Do you communicate honestly, without a personal agenda?

Gemini–Aquarius
RULED BY MERCURY AND SATURN/URANUS

This union is blessed right from the word *go* and has all the makings of a relationship that consistently whispers of magic. This mutual enchantment will endure for the duration of their connection and is likely to be a "forever" love if they are both willing to put in enough work.

Generally, there are two types of water bearers: one ruled by logical, conservative Saturn, and the other by unpredictable Uranus—although they are likely to protest their association with anything "general," stating, with indignance, that they are unlike anyone on Earth. This duality suits the Gemini twin very well because they have two (at the very least) dichotomous faces themselves.

The water bearer was ruled by Saturn long before Uranus was discovered, and this version is usually the more conservative, reserved type, able to commit to anything, or anyone, worthwhile and remain so for many moons.

Then there is the Uranian-ruled type, an unpredictable rebel. I call them the "wave makers" who are on a mission to wake us up from our inertia, greed, and ignorance. Wave makers struggle to commit because they are far too busy saving the planet to spend their precious energy on just one person. Unless that person is willing to walk the same path, they find it hard to settle, and the minute a lover displays possessiveness, or the uglier sides of a relationship emerge, they find the nearest escape route.

An Aquarius may flit between all of the above, but as a fixed sign, it's more likely that they find their path and stick to it, forcing everyone else to walk the same way or take the proverbial highway. And of course, they want to elevate the consciousness of every lover or friend (they're the same thing to an Aquarius) they have ever had, and, owing to their wanderlust natures, they likely have had more than a few.

Either way, both sides of Aquarius have a strong rebellious streak; a conscious, or unconscious, drive to evoke progress; and a burning desire to work for a cause bigger than just them.

The wave maker is less refined than the water bearer and may cause chaos and disruption just because they can. They fight against themselves, boredom, the norm, and anyone they rightly or wrongly perceive to be oppressing them or some other disadvantaged group. They never stay in one place for long enough to experience any real or nourishing intimacy. A Gemini can be very much the same, which is why at the moment they meet, there is a flash of recognition and an almost instant empathy. Whether they decide to pursue anything that lasts longer than that initial spark or not, the experience will be neither forgotten nor repeated.

TECHNICOLOR DREAMWORLD
When a Gemini and an Aquarius pause their dancing with the fairies and decide to bewitch each other, they see through each other's kaleidoscopic lens and know that this is no ordinary love. Finally,

it seems that these two unique beings have encountered another kindred spirit who understands their far-out views. They both know that outside this black-and-white (and sometimes dull and gray) existence, there is a technicolor dreamworld to explore.

Unless they have other more grounded planets close to their Sun signs (i.e., earth sign Moon/Mars/Saturn), or had restrictive upbringings or early traumas that hamper their free flow, they will buck social conventions and fall madly in love—and even more surprisingly for them, remain that way. Every day is brimming with opportunities to learn and grow.

They both have more layers to peel back than an onion, which keeps them interested in the other. The Gemini is enthralled by the sheer force of the Aquarius in their flow, as they manage to blend power with light and compassion. The Aquarius is delighted to be with a soul so similar yet different enough to offer a lifetime of discovery. Both are enchanted by the goodness that they know lies behind a cloak of wizardry and mischief. But the relationship is unlikely to ever get too relaxed or steady, and the moment one or both become complacent or too sure, the bombs will begin to drop on that love nest.

REACHING NIRVANA

These air signs have much in common, which is why this match has all the ingredients necessary for a soul mate union. Both desire independence, which doesn't mean they're incapable of fidelity or intimacy; it just means that they must be able to flourish within it and feel free. If that metaphorical door is left open, they will stay committed and loyal.

Each must support the other in growing and cultivating their light. The Gemini must embrace truth and cannot remain in an unevolved state of being. The Aquarius must execute patience and tolerance and show unconditional love, and the Gemini must appreciate that and invest equally.

As air signs, their incessant mental acrobatics require grounding through exercise and other healthy habits. Meditation and other forms of mind training will elevate their consciousness and deliver incredible results.

If both slow down and value the unique contribution their lover brings, this union will evolve toward new levels of intimacy and soul growth, on too many levels to list here.

If you are a Gemini who loves an Aquarius, contemplate the following:

✧ Do you encourage and support your lover?

✧ Do you treat your lover as you wish they would treat you?

✧ Do you feel free in this union?

✧ Does this relationship enhance your positive traits?

If you are an Aquarius who loves a Gemini, contemplate the following:

✧ Do you recognize the light in your lover? Do you magnify it?

✧ Are you willing to execute patience and unconditional love?

✧ Do you appreciate the fun side of your Gemini?

✧ Do you feel you can grow together?

Libra–Libra

RULED BY VENUS

Libra, the scales, is a masculine, cardinal sign. The latter usually indicates powerful leadership abilities, and this can be an oxymoron because Libras love to compromise, and peace and harmony are vital. If they are faced with constant tension or conflict, this can cause them to become unwell mentally and, at times, physically. They just can't handle it for long (unless they have Aries/Leo rising or Moon signs and delight in a good argument).

If both Libras gravitate more toward their star sign, this union has immense possibilities. But if one or both veer toward the unevolved manifestation of a Scorpio or a Virgo via their Moon, Venus, Mars, or rising signs, the partnership will overflow with control issues, jealousy, infidelity, and score-keeping. A Libra is all about fairness, balance, peace, and equality, so anything less may tickle their fancy for a short time, but long term, their souls will drive them to pull the rug on the relationship, consciously or subconsciously, and find something more harmonious.

A Libra is rarely alone for long, but the major lesson for them is to be comfortable in their own skin, to fall in love with themselves first. Unless they are seriously self-aware, they won't know that, though, and "next" is their go-to setting as they repeatedly attempt to satiate their insatiable desires (for pleasure on one level and real love on a soul level). When the two do meet, and if both have had enough of the conveyor belt of unsuitable lovers, they will try *hard* to make this work . . . and work it may.

Their ruling planet is the feminine Venus, so two scales combined are perhaps the most gender-fluid folks on Earth, able to swiftly flip between feminine and masculine personas and energy.

FAIRNESS FOR ALL

As a couple, two Libras are the epitome of compassionate love, charm, and fairness. Rarely are they divisive, preferring instead to heal rifts and help everyone get along, and often they will be the mediators in disputes. They take the time to assess the pros and cons of any words or actions, analyzing their lover's (and friends' and family's) behavior for both good and bad because they want to really understand what makes a person speak or act in a certain way. Such behavior imbues this love match with kindness and a solidarity that is soothing for each of them.

REACHING NIRVANA

Combining forces and working for a more inclusive society is a sure bet to keep these two growing as a couple. If they can do so professionally, this is even better. If not, then starting from where they are and working within their own lives and community is just as effective. This relationship must be balanced with both partners fully prepared to give and take in equal measure. If the scales tip, clear communication is key to restoring harmony.

Keeping the romance alive is also a prerequisite. Complacency harms any union, but for Libras combined, it's fatal.

Yoga is one of the best practices for these two to keep their yin and yang in equilibrium, and meditation will enable them to avoid the indecisiveness that is known to plague them.

If you are a Libra who loves another Libra, contemplate the following:

✧ Do you sacrifice your own needs for the sake of peace?

✧ Are you honest about what you want when you form a union?

✧ Do you listen to your inner voice? Do you listen to your partner?

✧ Try using daily meditation and train your mind to become a decisive, Jedi-like warrior.

Libra–Aquarius
RULED BY VENUS AND SATURN/URANUS

A Libra is romantic, and an Aquarius is far more logical yet fascinated by Libra's charm and diplomacy, which is something they often lack. This partnership begins with all the empathy, verve, and romance one might expect from two cerebral and emotionally intelligent air signs . . . and then descends into chaos if neither is evolved or they don't tread carefully.

On the surface, they have much in common: both strive for Utopia on Earth and are driven in bringing about a fair and equal society where all beings are respected and judged according to their virtue and character. But a Libra can be needy and push the buttons of their humanitarian lover, which triggers the rebellious wave maker to fight to become free and/or question their beliefs, morals, and integrity.

An Aquarius has strong opinions, but rarely will they 'fess up to their own shortcomings, preferring instead to cleverly argue and twist them into good qualities. When the wave maker is equally as aligned with the Saturn-ruled water bearer, they eventually will appreciate this sort of questioning and consider their impatience and, at times, anamorphic and selective compassion. A Libra will gently open their lover's mind and help them mature into the sincere, kind, and compassionate person they were starred to become. But if their ego resists, and it will, they will argue, fight, and engage in the one thing the Libra has refined to an art form: reasoned debate. When they lose the debate, the Aquarius will do what they do best and bounce, often leaving the million-dollar house, kids, and all other worldly possessions to the Libra without a backward glance, only stopping to gather any small animals.

Jokes aside, an Aquarius in their flow is not overly concerned with possessions or status (unless they have Capricorn, Leo, or Taurus influences) and will gladly give it all back in return for their freedom, which is only ever a state of mind as far as they are concerned. If their lover dares question their integrity or authenticity, even if it is questionable or inconsistent, then sheer indignance will push them to book a one-way ticket to volunteer at a faraway orphanage or sign up to work for a humanitarian aid group in a war-torn land—anything other than face the battles raging in their own home or heart.

Unless afflicted by Scorpio in their charts, neither holds grudges and both love each other enough to forgive and forget. Infidelity, which is betrayal as far as they are both concerned, is the exception to this, and neither is likely to remain committed to a stray unless it's the four-legged kind. A Libra plans to cohabit and do everything as a couple, and an Aquarius will "play house" for a time, but the Libra is likely to become offended when the Aquarius plans trips to climb Mount Everest alone or skip off to a silent meditation retreat. The Libra likes to do things together, and unless the water bearer has plenty of Libra in their charts, too, they like to feel free enough to explore solo. This can cause issues if the Libra takes this personally, but they shouldn't. Libras usually have mastered fair compromise; an Aquarius certainly has not.

SHARED IDEALS

These two are magnetized initially. They spend hours talking; sharing ideas; playing music; and discussing books, art, and opinions, and they are blown away by their similar ideals and dreams for a fairer society. A Libra holds this stance no matter what, but an Aquarius is less inclined to be tolerant if a person is corrupt, ignorant, bigoted, selfish, or lacking in morals. A Libra will delve into the person's background, examining the potential reasoning behind their behavior, and then deliver a fair course of action, which infuriates the intolerant wave maker, who thinks the Libra ought side with them, come what may.

On a positive note, the Aquarius often has ingenious ideas that serve a higher purpose, and the Libra will provide the structure and pragmatism to build a grounded framework, helping actualize the intangible, which delights the Aquarius to no end. For this reason, when they team up, they can turn lofty dreams into tangible reality.

REACHING NIRVANA

The Libra is usually the one to acquiesce and compromise for the sake of the union. They hold great love and understanding in their hearts for their contrary water bearer, but in the long term, a Libra requires balance, so the Aquarius must stay still and calm long enough to swallow their pride and listen to reason. An Aquarius is overflowing with compassion, but it needs to be evoked with an equally open heart. Open-hearted communication, self-reflection, the avoidance of blame, and mutual compromise are required for this union to evolve from a transient love affair into something lasting. Finding a just cause that encourages them to serve a higher purpose or others less fortunate is also a way to bind them together on a soul level.

If you are a Libra who loves an Aquarius, contemplate the following:

✧ Do you allow your lover to embark on solo adventures?

✧ Are you needy? If yes, can you reflect on this and compromise?

✧ What do you love about your water bearer?

✧ Do you have joint goals?

If you are an Aquarius who loves a Libra, contemplate the following:

✧ Do you compromise your need for independence with your lover's needs?

✧ Are you stubborn? If yes, is this pride, or the belief that you are always right?

✧ What do you appreciate about this union?

Aquarius–Aquarius
RULED BY SATURN AND URANUS

When these two meet, you can see the sparks flying from space— space being their natural habitat because any self-respecting wave maker/water bearer will readily confess to being part alien. (This is the sign of genius and insanity.) The two have an unspoken and instant bond and recognize the other as a trustworthy friend of old. Friendships come first for these two, and even though they are loyal to a fault, they are not comfortable with emotion (unless they have Cancer/Scorpio as a rising, Mercury, Venus, or Moon sign), preferring logic and rationale. They start out as friends, playfully testing each other's mental prowess, and if neither is found to be lacking, the seduction is stealthy and absolute.

The true water bearer is utterly unshockable, and this is the test: if they take offense easily, they fail the authenticity requirement, and the other will leave the conversation and eventually the union (at least mentally if not also physically). The match may have looked exceptional on paper, but now that they see the other is not a purebred alien, and they will never manage to seduce them into anything more intimate than friendship.

Many folks say they know an Aquarius, but the only other being that could ever know the water bearer is another water bearer. (This also may be true for a person with the same Moon sign/rising sign, or another planet in Aquarius, in their full natal charts.) It's fascinating to watch these two in action because they gently push each other's buttons, making outrageous statements and employing various other peculiar methods to ensure that their potential mate is as tolerant, open-minded, sincerely humanitarian, evolved, and worthy as they think they are.

Some signs will ignore red flags for the fear of being alone, but not Aquarius. They don't do fear because they know this life is only one of many, and another incarnation is a sure bet. When something doesn't work out, they simply shrug and move on. They may try again, but eventually they will walk away in full confidence that if a soul mate union fails in this life, they have plenty of others so it's not a big deal.

Both enjoy being alone and are rarely lonely. They don't care about the societal or parental pressure to settle down—the thought of that expectation actually offends them. Yet together, they respect each other's sole pursuits and space, which is hard for other signs, who take it as rejection or cold indifference. They'll only consider sacrificing their independence if the other person has self-awareness, compassion, and empathy as a driving force. Some signs will take that risk. But contrary to their easygoing reputations, Aquarians will not enter a commitment lightly. When they make promises, they do all they can to keep them, so they are often cautious in that respect.

FAITHFUL

An Aquarius has an eclectic collection of friends, and some may be lovers or past lovers. The evolved among them care little for gender, status, race, or creed; they fall in love with souls or minds, so why would any of that surface stuff matter? They tolerate anyone as long as they have good hearts and intentions. As a couple, two Aquarians are freedom fighters. They are extreme and fanatical at the worst, but at the best, they are gently opening bigoted hearts and minds because they see the fear behind hatred and intolerance.

When they commit, being unfaithful is not an option. If they are, they are not authentically Aquarian. They offer and expect respect, trust, and honesty. For that reason, if they do decide to jump in, they are all in and will work hard to maintain a healthy union that honors the other's right to grow. Boundaries are clear, and disputes are settled with compassion and kindness. When it works well, it's an exciting match with the potential to win over the most detached airhead and bring them back to earth for long enough to build a lasting partnership, although not one likely to follow the norm. For these two to conform to society's perception of normal would feel like an utter betrayal.

Aquarius–Aquarius are popular as a couple and enjoy socializing and going on wild adventures that usually involve a plan to rescue those in need or maybe arrest whale-killing pirates. Whatever the case, although life was never dull, when they team up, it becomes an action-packed experience that lasts as long as they do.

REACHING NIRVANA

These two are usually evolved, attuned beings who are born on this earth to raise vibrations and show other mortals how to build an enlightened society. For that reason, they prefer to live unconventional lives. They know on a profound level that here, in the West, we have more people on antidepressants than anywhere else for good reason.

Both are prone to suffer from overstimulation and burnout, which is why they are more likely to call remote retreats, tree houses, and off-the-grid communities home than a terraced house with a cute garden and white picket fence.

Meditation and unplugging from the daily bombardment of information is essential to both the longevity of this union and their sanity.

If you are an Aquarius who loves another Aquarius, contemplate the following:

✧ Do you two have a common cause? If yes, great. If not, find one to bind you and get you on track with your life's mission.

✧ Do you unplug regularly? If not, you need to do so to protect each other's energy, which is always on and receiving.

✧ Do you meditate? If not, you must learn how to tame your mind and attune to higher consciousness.

Fire and Water Signs Combined
Aries–Cancer
RULED BY MARS AND THE MOON

The ram and the crab! You may wonder how this is going to work—they wonder that, too, but that won't stop them trying. The ram feels that the Cancer is the one, and when they set their sights on their paramour, that's it. But unless the ram has water signs in their charts or can speak "crab" (some can, but they are very few and far between), they are lacking in emotional intelligence. Just like newborn babies, they want what and who they want, and they want it *now*—patience is not their strong suit. Rams will point-blank refuse to slow down, read between the lines, or follow the signs because those are nudges from the universe and one's own intuition, and the ram is often blind to the signs and immune to emotion—unless, of course, it's their own, in which case, how dare anyone be insensitive. The only time either is likely to arise for the ram is when they are not getting their own way.

Both creatures are masters of passive aggression, and when not in their flow, they can be fixed in their beliefs and dead set on getting their own way. The crab likely will trigger the ram's melodramatics and then sit there looking innocent or wail a woeful tune of self-pity. If they are not careful, this shows the danger signs of a karmic battle that will last for lifetimes. On the flip side, evolved crabs don't like drama. They appreciate peace, tranquility, and time to sit on the beach making sandcastles.

The ram is on a mission. They are energetic and forceful, unless they are more mature in years and exhausted by the rejections of life or otherwise evolved and at peace within their own heart. Then, and only then, will this union turn into something magic. Compromise is the key.

MINDFUL INTERACTIONS

The answer comes when both tread carefully and have patience with the other. The Aries must chill out and stop trying to force the crab into doing everything their way, and the crab needs to communicate openly before they reach the point of manipulative behavior or explosions.

Regardless of gender, we all display feminine and masculine tendencies during different times and situations in our lives, and the ram, who gravitates more toward the masculine vibe of Aries, is often heroic. These born leaders will defend those who are vulnerable, without a thought for their own safety or comfort. When they encounter a crab, they feel an almost instant surge of empathy and want to take care of them, which is exactly how the crab likes it.

The crab, in its flow, is stalwart and also will fight to the death to defend and protect their loved ones, but they are not overly impressed with the ram's relentless pursuit for more—more happiness, more money, more adventure. They find the ram exhausting and will retreat into their shell to escape. This infuriates the ram if they're looking to fight, if not physically then with lethal words.

But Cancer remembers every single utterance, including punctuation, and if you wound them, they will hold on to that for eternity. So after one Mars-fueled message or tirade of fury too many, they are likely to leave the ram. The ram will sense that they are losing, and this will infuriate them even more. If they are bound together for familial or professional reasons and the Cancer has withdrawn in any way, the anger that simmers beneath the Aries's smile is palpable and destructive.

REACHING NIRVANA
This is not an easy love match; however, I have known this coupling to be happy and successful (i.e., harmonious, balanced, and enduring) when the ram has a prominent planet in Cancer (rising/Moon/Venus/Mars). Cancer will be much more tolerant of the ram's neuroses if they have an Aries placement in their charts, too.

The relationship can work well if both love each other enough to work at it, if the Aries is not overly preoccupied with self, and if the Cancer is forgiving and patient. Neither must be too focused on material success and worldly gain; this is not the path toward enlightenment.

Facing their own flaws will help them grow, and they both need a sense of humor, lightness, and unconditional love. A mutual desire for self-improvement will help each gain an understanding of the other. Meditation is helpful for us all, but reflective spiritual practice will ensure these two commit to the union, and to loving each other, for many lifetimes.

If you are an Aries who loves a Cancer, contemplate the following:

✧ Are you honest with your lover?

✧ Do you feel that you compromise?

✧ Do you take your partner's sensitivity into consideration?

If you are a Cancer who loves an Aries, contemplate the following:

✧ Do you secretly admire your ram's tenacity? If yes, then praise them.

✧ Do you take responsibility for your own feelings and emotional well-being?

✧ Are you overly sensitive?

Aries–Scorpio
RULED BY MARS AND MARS/PLUTO

This challenging union requires equal amounts of mutual devotion and maturity if it is to work in the long term.

The initial chemistry between the ram and scorpion is likely to go one of two ways, and which way depends entirely on their levels of self-awareness and spirituality. If they know themselves, understand the laws of karma and cause and effect, and bravely face their weaknesses without blame, this relationship can be astonishing. They are the original power couple, and if others don't want to *be* them, they will certainly flock *to* them in the hope that some of their energy will rub off.

It works well if the Aries gravitates toward more of a masculine energy and the Scorpio, a feminine. This is because the former is on a journey to learn how to become more emotionally mature and intelligent, and when the Scorpio combines their own power over the emotional realms with softer feminine characteristics, the union is more balanced, evolved, and loving. When both are open and able to work through their high levels of attachment and desire, they can build a lasting relationship, keeping them both on their toes yet committed to each other.

The Aries is magnetized by the Scorpio and helpless in submitting to their power and sexual allure. They will readily commit and happily practice what doesn't come so naturally: fidelity. Aries are generally refreshingly honest, and if they do stray, rarely is it premeditated—more likely a spur-of-the-moment passion. However, they are the first to confess so they can do what they do best: move on, whether alone or with their Scorpio. An Aries will at least readily attempt to forgive and forget, but although a Scorpio eventually forgives, they never forget. If an Aries is unfaithful, they may as well have lit a stick of dynamite under the house. A Scorpio, although known to partake in extramarital liaisons, is more likely to indulge in clandestine affairs. An Aries will make excuses for their lover's infidelity—which is futile, because then the Scorpio starts to lose all respect for this accepting version of their ram and partakes in even more public betrayals until eventually the union goes up in flames.

CHEMISTRY

Mars is the planet of war and, therefore, springtime belongs to Aries, the season the Romans believed yielded the best results in battle. An Aries likes to go in ardently and fast, aiming only to win. A Scorpio, meanwhile, is the ruler of winter and darkness, with most of their battles being covert, preplanned, and deadly.

A chemical reaction like theirs doesn't have to be violent or hazardous, but it can be. If this coupling goes awry, the Scorpio will spew forth toxic gases because that's what they do to poison the enemy. The Aries then will burst into flames, which means people inevitably will get hurt. This may sound extreme, and if the ram has more calming signs in their full chart or the Scorpio has a strong sense of purpose and self-esteem, all will be well. But these two are likely to be anything other than stable or peaceful for long.

Their passion is irrefutable, and if they are evolved, there is no stronger alliance or combined sheer force of will that can right the wrongs of humanity, shine a torch on the greedy and ignorant, defend the vulnerable, and build an enchanting life based on service to humanity. If they are not evolved, they will use their combined might for selfish purposes, to gain status and power, and to destroy any obstacles or people, imagined or real, they perceive to be in their way. It's terrifying.

Both are strong beyond belief, but the Aries is skilled in spontaneous action and prefers swift results so they can perform their victory dance all the way home. The Scorpio, on the other hand, is a master of strategy, patience, and annihilation.

If the Aries has been wounded by a past or early life trauma, they can be more defensive than the Cancer, and that's exhausting for any of the other signs to deal with for long. They attack their own shadow until they work themselves into a frenzy and burn out. And now this is where it gets interesting: the Scorpio sees beyond the front into the shining heart of the Aries and helps them calm down. An Aries is probably the only one who will ever feel truly safe with a Scorpio. They have courage and a strong enough sense of self to hold their own in any battle, and a Scorpio loves to fight for a cause—if there isn't one, they create one. This can be incredible, or devastating, and rarely is there any in-between.

REACHING NIRVANA

These two thrive on passion, which we all know eventually will die out. But when each can recognize the contribution the other is bringing to their lives, they will put in the work needed to ensure a happy life together.

Spirituality is key, and understanding the workings of the world, karma, and cause and effect will prevent them from going back and forth with useless, negative patterns of behavior, like blame, defensiveness, and getting even.

The Scorpio is offered many chances to learn a major life lesson, forgiveness. For that reason, the Aries is their supreme copilot. The latter loves to feel free, and they know that any harboring of resentments and grudges slows them down, all of which they unbegrudgingly teach the Scorpio. The Scorpio is mastering emotional intelligence and wisdom, which the Aries greatly benefits from. This makes for a lively union, and growth, as a theme, will help bond them for life.

If you are an Aries who loves a Scorpio, contemplate the following:

✧ Do you take your lover's feelings into consideration?

✧ Do you have anger tantrums (internal or external)? If so, this is toxic, so get some help.

✧ Try not to be too preoccupied with self, and think of your lover's needs, too.

✧ Does your Scorpio make you feel jealous? If yes, reflect on why.

✧ Do you try to evolve your soul? If so, how?

If you are a Scorpio who loves an Aries, contemplate the following:

✧ Do you play mind games?

✧ Are you patient without a personal agenda?

✧ Do you appreciate your ram's courage, spice, and all things nice?

✧ Do you suffer from jealousy? If yes, this is a poison. You need to examine the triggers and work on the reasons why.

✧ Study the law of karma, cause and effect, and impermanence, which will help you elevate your consciousness above purely worldly desires.

Aries–Pisces
RULED BY MARS AND JUPITER/NEPTUNE

A ram and a fish together sounds biblical, and this union certainly can make both feel as if it was foretold by an ancient prophet. These two are drawn to each other in ways that defy logic. On the surface, they make strange bedfellows, yet the Pisces has a superpower wrapped in gentleness that cuts through that surface, taking the Aries on an emotional journey into the depths of love and offering a rare chance for them to experience senses they didn't even know they possessed.

The Aries, in return, shows the fish how danger can be converted to opportunity when you exert enough courage. The Pisces secretly fears being out of control yet yearns to lose themselves, and the Aries secretly wishes they could escape being themselves, even just for one day. So these two provide a safety net of differences that holds them steady.

The Aries has the potential to coax the Pisces into a commitment that is both solid and dreamy, and the Pisces helps the Aries slow down long enough to get to know each star in the sky and appreciate the flowers blooming in the garden. The flowers have been there since they moved in ten years ago and the stars, well, for eternity, but when the Aries joins hands with their Pisces, they notice the magic in simplicity and nature in ways they never had before.

Aries is a masculine sign and vibe, and unless they have strong Pisces signs in planets in their full natal charts, they will aggressively hunt down everything they want with a strong forward march. Pisces, on the other hand, is more fluid. They take the time to first assess the climate and then make slow strides toward the object of their desire or affection. This changes if the Pisces has a fire sign Moon or rising sign; in that case, they will switch quickly from assertion to compliance. One may never know which mood they are in, which keeps the Aries keen and interested, as they secretly love a challenge. This rule is overwritten for a ram with a Cancer Moon/Venus or rising sign, in which case, they eventually just want to settle into something stable—but it still must be interesting.

An Aries will tell you they are sensitive at heart, and this may be true, but that sensitivity only surfaces when someone has offended their ego or their loved ones, who they often see as an extension of themselves; so it's back to *me*, *my*, or *I*. They don't mean to be so caught up in themselves; they just rarely chill for long enough to engage in any serious self-reflection, which is where the fish in their positive flow comes to the rescue. The Pisces can gently awaken the ram and make them want to become a better, more thoughtful person.

Don't be fooled by the fish. They actually are far more controlling than the ram, which is a trait they have in common with their opposite sign, Virgo. Pisces just do it in a much more creative fashion: they disappear, play the victim, feign hurt, or push the ram's buttons and then they have won. The ram feels awful and spends the next few hours bending over backward to apologize. You see the game? And trust me, it is a game.

COOPERATION

An Aries must learn to cooperate in any union, but for these two, it is essential. To take a back seat is not their usual practice, but in partnership with a Pisces, when they learn to respect the art of the subtle and take into consideration their lover's communication and feelings, their stars align.

In return, the secretive fish cannot expect this partnership to be calm and cohesive if they hide things from their ram, which will lead to all sorts of trouble. We can all dial in to masculine and feminine energy, and a Pisces with an Aries is a balanced match when they can temper their assertiveness with gentleness. If the Pisces has yet to crack the former, the Aries can teach them exactly how, and how not, to master that one, and vice versa.

The Aries has a bad reputation in love. They are perceived as unfaithful—and they, like all the signs, can be—but when they decide they have met the one, they jump in fully.

The Pisces usually has many potential options but can be very fussy. They will accept the attention but slip away before any expectations are set to catch them.

REACHING NIRVANA

At heart, both are romantics, so when they pair up, they open a Pandora's box of delights. They show their love and affection in different yet harmonious ways and complement each other.

Both benefit on a soul level through self-reflection and a desire to improve. Meditation, prayer, and a strong spiritual practice will bond them, making them stronger both as a couple and individually.

If the Aries learns acceptance and the Pisces avoids playing the victim, all will be well, enabling these two to build a fantasy castle far from prying eyes or predators.

If you are an Aries who loves a Pisces, contemplate the following:

✧ Do you appreciate the gentle side of yourself when you're with your lover?

✧ Does this union help you chill out?

✧ Do you have a short fuse? If so, examine the triggers and be sure they are not ego based.

If you are a Pisces who loves an Aries, contemplate the following:

✧ Do you play the martyr? If so, examine the reasons why, and try to stop.

✧ What do you love about your Aries? List the reasons.

✧ Do you express, and own, your emotions without blame?

Sagittarius–Cancer
RULED BY JUPITER AND THE MOON

When the archer meets the crab, so begins a mambo style of dance that merrily leads them into each other's arms and hearts—eventually.

This is a union based on soul growth, one brimming with the potential for mutual, major transformation on profound levels.

This duo has so much to gain and learn from each other. The crab makes the archer's little heart sing with glee because their thirst for knowledge (rivaled only by that of its opposite sign, Gemini) is as inexhaustible as their need for adventure. The evolved crab has invented an impressive blend of sensitivity and wisdom, which makes them incredible partners and stand-up human beings. They are aware that without real wisdom, sensitivity is simply self-attachment, which triggers the trap of defensiveness of the lower ego. Many mistakenly think that ego is arrogance and pride, but in the real umbrella sense of the word, it is a preoccupation with self.

This union will last only if the crab is evolved, or at the very least attempting not to take this life so seriously, as well as realizing that not every word or action delivered to them by the world is aimed at hurting them. In any case, a union with an unevolved version of the defensive crab exhausts the archer's patience and has them running to the nearest hill or airport, whichever takes them the farthest away, fast. Equally, the crab will sidestep away from an archer who is lacking in self-awareness or basic kindness. They are few and far between, but they do exist.

The evolved archer knows they are somewhat lacking in tact and diplomacy, with their uncompromising delivery of truth, which is often a somewhat skewed version anyway. One lesson they must attempt to master in this lifetime is empathy. No human can do this without wanting to understand, and share in, the feelings of another. Feelings! Now there is a new concept for the Sagittarius. Sure, they know all about indignance, fury, and self-righteousness, but empathy? That takes time. They don't set out to hurt people's feelings, but they often have an uncompromising attitude, especially when their ruler, Jupiter the "judge," runs amok and they believe you somehow deserved it. All this is second nature to the archer until they fall in love with their crab. That is when they stop aiming the arrow; cock their head to one side; and pay attention to how their actions, words, and blustering behavior impacts their gentle lover. Then they will try and try again until they hit that harmonic note, which sounds like angels singing in the heavens. This relationship can be brilliant for both if curiosity, respect, and patience allow them to talk things through with a spirit of compromise and without blame.

Crabs are the caretakers of the zodiac; they have an instinct to provide emotional comfort for others, which is a beauty to behold and a pleasure to encounter. When a crab sympathizes with you, you can feel it warming you through to your bones. But there are those who give with certain expectations of a return, and when those returns are not given, they become snippy, argumentative, and bitter.

MUTUAL GROWTH

Nobody, not even a crab, stands a chance of reaching beyond the surface of their own bottomless well of emotion. The whimsical and unsuspecting archer is clueless when it comes to Cancer's still waters running deep behind a gentle demeanor, which makes it even more interesting when the crab offers them a glimpse, and totally bewildering when they snap.

The archer is learning the power of the spoken word, and although noncrab people will protest that sticks and stones (or any blunt objects) are the only tools able to hurt others, a love match with a crab will soon show the archer just how wrong that thought is. Together they will grow closer, stronger, and surer.

REACHING NIRVANA

Communication, without the need for rights or wrongs, is required for a union to survive. These two are very different beings, and unless the Cancer has a Sagittarius planet, or the Sagittarius has a Cancer planet, they are going to have to work hard to explain themselves without becoming emotionally pent up.

The archer needs to soften their approach and examine the ways in which they communicate and how that can sometimes be hurtful. The Cancer must know that hardly anything is entirely personal; it's more about where the other person is in terms of their soul growth. Spiritual practice is the revitalizing tonic for these two, however they choose to do that. Yoga, meditation, prayer, and retreats all work wonderfully.

If you are a Sagittarius who loves a Cancer, contemplate the following:

✧ Mindfulness was invented for archers, who speak first and think later. Try hard to practice the reverse. It will help every relationship you have.

✧ Try to slow down and take your lover's feelings into consideration.

✧ Regular exercise is the way for you to enhance mind, body, and spiritual balance.

✧ Meditate.

If you are a Cancer who loves a Sagittarius, contemplate the following:

✧ Try not to take your archer's words to heart, especially if they are blunt or reactive. Instead, look at their actions.

✧ Do you take responsibility for your own feelings?

✧ Are you prepared to work on your ingrained tendency to take things too personally?

Sagittarius–Scorpio
RULED BY JUPITER AND MARS/PLUTO

If you read the mythology behind the archer's name and symbol on page 50, you will recall that they are depicted with a drawn bow and an arrow aimed directly at Scorpio's heart, should the latter need to be taken out quickly. The archer feels compelled to restrain Scorpio, keeping them in check and calling them out on any behaviors that could be considered salacious.

At first, the Scorpio is prone to eye up the archer as prey or a transient plaything . . . until they fall in love, which only happens if the Sagittarius is deemed savvy and educated and never, ever airs their dirty laundry in public. Archers ought to take note: they cannot continue blustering their way through life if they treasure the union they are creating. Discretion and privacy are as vital to this relationship's longevity as love, and if the archer wants to stay alive, they would be wise to put their brain in gear before engaging their foghorns. If they don't, they will be frozen out of any intimacies with the Scorpio.

Unless the archer has Scorpio in their chart, they will be open, honest, happy-go-lucky adventurers with trusting natures, and if they believe the Scorpio to be a good yet misguided being, they will stay and prevent the Scorpio from making decisions that may have serious karmic repercussions, like destroying a colleague's reputation if they pose a threat or manipulating their ailing grandma into signing over the entirety of her fortune. In short, the Sagittarius acts as the moral compass the Scorpio doesn't always have, and unless they have worked hard on self-awareness, they don't. This also goes for those with planets like Venus/Moon/Jupiter/Mars in Scorpio; the goodness *is* there, it's just often tightly wrapped in their warped perception that everyone is an enemy until proven otherwise. The annihilation of anyone who poses a threat is second nature to the Scorpio, who stings first and (perhaps) regrets later. Death or cancellation of the opposition is the only option as far as they are concerned. The archer provides a wise sounding board and is often uncannily aware of the laws of karma and cause and effect, which helps stop the Scorpio in their locked-on laser-beam quest for control and power.

BALANCE

A Scorpio delights in their archer's enthusiasm and optimism, which is often in stark contrast to their own overanalytical minds and suspicious natures. All of this is overruled if the Scorpio is evolved or has a rising sign or planet like Venus, Mercury, or the Moon in Sagittarius; likewise for the Sagittarius, in which case their boundless zest for life is dialed down and replaced with brooding. The Scorpio, with a helping of Sagittarius in their natal chart, is given an exuberant skip in their step.

The archer and scorpion are a great match because when they combine, they balance and ground each other's instabilities and shortcomings. This leads to a greater awareness of self, and life is seen more as an adventure than a score-keeping chore.

If the archer is a pure-born Sagittarius, they want to feel free and won't tolerate jealousy, possessiveness, or any sort of conduct that could be perceived as controlling. It's not always unjustified, though, because the unevolved archer is a philanderer, which won't wash with the Scorpio, who is fearful of betrayal and disgusted by disloyalty.

If the Sagittarius is truly *all in*, they may stay and try to reason with their green-eyed Scorpio, but indignance soon takes over if the Scorpio has poisoned themselves with the above, and then it's impossible. The archer sees through this Scorpionic behavior and will work to assure their loyalty for a time. But if they are getting nowhere, they usually leave with heavy hearts. Likewise, if the Scorpio believes the archer is lacking in devotion, intelligence, or ambition, they will begin looking for their next unsuspecting victim.

REACHING NIRVANA

Both need to leave the past behind and build a fresh and clean future. If infidelity is or has been an issue, this is harder to get past for the Scorpio than the archer, who has a more understanding nature. Forgiveness is the biggest life lesson for a Scorpio, and life loves them so much that it offers them many opportunities to practice this in the guise of personal and professional relationships. An evolved Scorpio works on their own issues and has an endless well of sympathy and empathy. They open their heart and mind to their lover, and when they commit and take a vow, officially or in secret, to love and support the archer in times of joy and adversity, it's forever. This level of commitment and respect provides the Sagittarius with a love and acceptance unlike any match they have encountered before.

Honesty is a trait assigned to the archer, but that needs to be combined with discernment and trust. Honesty is the only policy these two need to agree on.

Taking refuge in a higher vision and practicing spirituality and clean living is the way this union will flourish and endure. Both will eventually realize that pure love is as close to God as they will ever get.

If you are a Sagittarius who loves a Scorpio, contemplate the following:

✧ Do you honor the depth of feeling your Scorpio has?

✧ Do you judge your lover harshly?

✧ Are you faithful? If yes, does your lover trust you and vice versa? If yes, this is an evolved union!

✧ Are you able to accept your lover as they are?

If you are a Scorpio who loves a Sagittarius, contemplate the following:

✧ How easy is it for you to trust?

✧ If you have been hurt in the past, can you let go of that pain and see the perpetrator as your teacher?

✧ Do you respect your archer?

✧ What do you appreciate about your lover?

Sagittarius–Pisces
RULED BY JUPITER AND JUPITER/NEPTUNE

And so joineth the archer and the fish. Or on a bad day, a self-righteous infidel and self-flagellating martyr—I'm sure you can guess which is which. Although I'm half-joking, the humor is laced with potent truth. A Sagittarius, as the ultimate truth-seeker, doesn't stop their search for the meaning behind life, God, and the universe on Earth. They go far beyond on their journey to find reason, and when they believe they've discovered what they think is the truth, the preacher is born and everyone else must listen to them. Luckily, the fish, in full flow, is a born listener; they try to empathize, sympathize, and understand their archer, who will struggle to find someone who wants to hear what they have to say and values their opinions. These opinions can be enlightened, if they have traveled through far-flung lands, studying the native cultures and faiths, which means that their deductions are educated or at the very least informed, if not altogether correct. But it's pointless ever telling them they are wrong.

The fish rewrites history with themselves as the persecuted one, and this drives the archer mad. Archers are 100 percent intolerant of people who dwell in suffering or paint a picture that fails to denote their favorite friend, truth. Fish have a colorful track record with that one.

Then we have our gracious and almost always beautiful Pisces martyr, who secretly dreams of finding a soul mate union and a higher vision that ignites faith, be that through spirituality or religion, and to be at one with the universe and all beings.

The thousands of client charts I've interpreted have indicated that these two have a strong karmic connection, and one that works very well at times, with a comforting, instant flash of recognition. But it's rarely comfortable for long. Perhaps they reunited to work through some past-life issues or to finally form something enduring. Only their souls would be able to tell you the answer to that one. I do know that those with certain Sagittarius alignments of planets (mainly to Neptune, the ruler of Pisces) have, in one lifetime or another, embarked on crusades as defenders of some sort of faith, sworn to fight for one religion or another. And in past lives, fish have taken vows of celibacy and sacrifice to align with their faith, commune with their perception of God, and pray for all our salvation.

In this life, this soul memory leads to the archer either finding peace and meaning in their own version of spiritual truth or adopting an attitude of total nihilism. Either way, you'll know exactly where they stand because they are never shy in voicing their beliefs or nonbeliefs.

COMPATIBILITY

The fish, if working in full flow in their sign, still manages to make sacrifices for others. Graciously, or begrudgingly, they are natural healers who can fix the broken wings of fragile birds only to watch forlornly as they fly away. It's hard being a fish in that respect, but they have their mission in life, and it's not one of self-serving or selfishness. In their next incarnation, they are likely to be born under the next neighboring sign, which is Aries, and then they can pretty much march to the beat of their own drum. For now, like their opposite sign, Virgo, it's all about service. If they can avoid feeling victimized or sorry for their lot, their kindness brings the greatest rewards of all.

When the stars align and these two meet, the fish is dazzled by the clever, exciting archer, who has an innate strength and sense of purpose. The archer is the zodiac's defender of truth and keeper of the faith—exactly what faith that is we can't say for certain, but when they encounter a fish, archers are enchanted by such gentleness of spirit, which has the calming effect of a waterfall.

REACHING NIRVANA

In short, mutual respect and tolerance must be ever present. Yet it is faith and a love of culture and the arts that can divide or bind these two. Without it, it could be a testy union.

If they each hold the intention of offering the other pure love, both will become empowered in ways that benefit them and everyone else they may encounter.

If the archer is spiritually inclined, they will respect the views of their fish, even if they differ. If they are not, they may verbally bully the fish into submission until their faith begins to wane and they feel lost. The fish must not slip into victim mode, but if they need to retreat, that's okay. They must explain to the rational archer that they need faith in some higher vision, and then together these two can build something superlative.

The archer must practice mindfulness, and if the fish develops the courage of their convictions, this will keep them both interested and keen to please the other. Prayer, retreat, and perhaps studying the old texts of sages and prophets is a smart move for both. The fish knows it all in the hidden recesses of their wise mind, and the archer *believes* they know; when they read spiritual wisdom in black and white, they both can process its supreme meaning and have a commonality to debate, which is music to the archer's hard-of-hearing ears.

The fish teaches the archer fluidity and acceptance, and in return, the fish gains confidence and reasoned wisdom.

If you are a Sagittarius who loves a Pisces, contemplate the following:

✧ Do you push your opinions onto your fish?

✧ How do you define faith?

✧ Are your opinions educated?

✧ Do you know how to relax?

✧ Are you kind to yourself?

If you are a Pisces who loves a Sagittarius, contemplate the following:

✧ Do you often help others? If so, do you know when to retreat?

✧ What does faith mean to you?

✧ Does your archer inspire you? If yes, have you told them?

✧ Is your soul gentle? If yes, honor that and avoid toxic, harsh people or words.

Leo–Cancer
RULED BY THE SUN AND THE MOON

When the noble and mighty lion meets a strong yet soft-shelled crab, they tickle and rub each other's tender underbellies for eternity. It could be like that because this pair has incredible potential as a couple, with the capacity to create a star-blessed and lasting union . . . *if*—and that's a big *if*—they have worked to become self-aware and are kind and evolved. In that case, past-life soul memory gives the Leo the instant ability to sympathize, tolerate (mostly), and understand the crab's ever-changing moods and irksome ways, helping them become a devoted partner and fierce public defender of their crabby friend or lover. In return, the emotionally intelligent Cancer misses nothing and will adore the lion 'til death do they part.

Adoration is just how a Leo likes (if not *needs*) love to be. That said, a Leo will almost always become infuriated because a Cancer is prone to going missing in action, emotionally, physically, or both. Lions need not take it so personally, but they do. A Cancer won't be available to hear the minutiae of every outrage and injustice the lion has had to face in a day, from the rude customer service representative who dared keep them on hold to the neighbor who stole their parking space. It's easy for a logical sign like an Aquarius to zone out, or a Pisces to disappear into the tune inside their head, but a Cancer is the psychic sponge of the zodiac and they can't easily escape being sucked into the drama.

For this union to last longer than a season, the Leo must understand that the Cancer needs those pockets of time alone to replenish their vitality and chi. The Leo ought to spread out those drama dumps among the rest of their friends and family—or better yet, let them go and move on. I am not saying all lions are like this. In fact, the noble Leo is more likely than most to fight major injustices through causes and the courts, but they also have the tendency to replay slights or other inconsequential trivia again and again, and this doesn't sit well with a Cancer. They suck it all up for a while, internalize it all, and then have a mighty meltdown.

Upon inspection, it is generally the evolved crab who is the ultimate protector of this union. They quietly guard the security, emotions, and overall well-being of their lion, which helps make this duo a cohesive team who easily succeed materially and will wipe out any opposition. The Leo will likely command from the front, with all eyes on them, but the Cancer strategizes all the moves. People wrongly assume that the Cancer is the more submissive, but that is only until there is a threat to their security or someone messes with their friends or family. Then, it's all-out war. They get down and dirty in the emotional mud and usually win the battle for supremacy. You will see a warring Leo coming a mile away—first the battle cry, swiftly followed by the pomp and ceremony—but like fellow water sign Scorpio, you won't see a crab coming until the sting or sideswipe is fatal.

EGO AND LOWER EGO

This union is transformative for good and for bad. If you study both the lion's and crab's natal charts and don't find any strong stamps of Cancer in the lion's chart (i.e., a planet, rising sign, or midheaven) or stamps of Leo in the Cancer's chart, long-term success might be more challenging. The only way the lack of empathy or commonality will be overridden is through reflective work and effective spiritual practice.

The Leo must work on their self-centeredness and ego-fueled pride, and the crab needs to realize that sensitivity is lower ego in disguise as something nicer. So let's clear this up once and for all: sensitivity is ego triggered by taking someone else's words or actions personally. (And it's exhausting!) That's when defensiveness kicks in. The *only* time sensitivity is helpful is when it's married to wisdom and then, and only then, is it activated via empathy, feeling, and compassion for other beings and nothing to do with self. Both Cancer and Leo, not flowing well, adopt the low-vibe mafia attitude of, "It's my family against the rest of the world." So when these two unite, it can magnify this "them versus us" mentality. If that happens, they seek out external battles to win. When those run out, wars rage within the walls of their own closed hearts and ballooned egos.

Forgive me, Cancer and Leo readers, but please keep going because this is important. If you have ever studied spiritual law, and even if you haven't, what I am about to say should resonate on a soul level. We have all been on this planet so many times that every being has been your lover or your mother. We are all family. Fighting against or not forgiving one of us is only hurting yourself in the long run. Contemplating the laws of impermanence and karma, cause, and effect will help you grow into the fabulous beings you were destined to become. Forgive others and yourselves and move on. Life is short, and it's a game. But this game of life is never one to be *won*; it's merely a game of self-improvement.

Lions are powerful by design, but if they are insecure, they are more likely than not to become obsessed with themselves and have little interest in building anything more than an army of sycophantic fans. The Cancer is not one to feign affection for anyone for too long, especially if the lion is too grandiose or arrogant. The crab will only endure a lover's preoccupation with self if they are providing for them on some level. So if that annoying tendency provides a huge house, clothes sent by a stylist each season, and their own cave with locks on the doors, they will stay, for security and convenience's sake.

All that is overruled if the Cancer has strong placements in Aquarius or Leo. In that case, no price is enough for their freedom. Unless the lion becomes the openhearted, generous, confident, and loving being they were born to be, the Cancer will scurry off to the nearest sandcastle and wait for the tide to take them far away, leaving the lion licking its wounded pride, roaring to anyone who will listen.

REACHING NIRVANA

Most lions and crabs have a great sense of humor, and as a couple, they are going to need it to overcome the massive helpings of ego and pride that both possess. Laughing at life, together, is the best way. In that humor lies great wisdom, as everything is impermanent and all pain is transient, as is pleasure, so don't take it all too seriously. Sincerely? Yes. But never too seriously.

These two are here to serve, as are we all, but both must overcome the habit of serving only themselves and those they love. For this reason, practicing meditation, finding an authentic teacher, and studying the higher mind will be important. Then together they will be able to make strides toward progress. We all need guidance in this world of illusion, and walking hand-in-hand with a soul mate is a true blessing.

If you are a Leo who loves a Cancer, contemplate the following:

✧ Do you take it personally when your crab needs space? If so, stop that!

✧ Do you and you lover laugh often? It's important to have humor in your lives.

✧ Do you listen to your partner and intuit their needs? And they yours?

If you are a Cancer who loves a Leo, contemplate the following:

✧ Do you criticize your lover? If so, try unconditional love instead.

✧ Are you able to communicate your feelings without becoming defensive?

✧ Do you know how or when to heal your energy?

Leo–Scorpio

RULED BY THE SUN AND MARS/PLUTO

A lion and a scorpion—that sounds fun! . . . said nobody ever.

This coupling comes with a cautionary warning sign. These two are more compatible when the Leo is the more masculine of the couple and the Scorpio gravitates toward a feminine vibe. That way, the power flows equally between yin and yang and neither feels threatened, which can lead to the sort of earthly chaos that sends shock waves down to the Scorpio's natural habitat, the underworld.

The Leo generally assumes the leadership in this relationship, and the Scorpio is content to assert their power more quietly. The Scorpio prefers to be financially in control, but money isn't usually an issue for a besotted lion who is more easygoing and generous with the Scorpio than they are with any of the other signs. The Leo is hypnotized by the scorpion's charisma, which is quite unlike their own charms.

This union takes a lot of work. (But don't they all?) Patience, understanding, and mutual tolerance must flow freely because the partners are *so* different from each other. However, one ever-present commonality that's as ever present as their sexual chemistry is control—they both need it. This may lead to dirty fights, infidelity, and battles for supremacy. Nobody will ever know who wins those fights because these two have very different interpretations of victory. The Leo stands proud in the knowledge that they were right and even crows about their conquest all over town. Meanwhile, the Scorpio has closed the joint accounts, changed the locks and phone numbers, and packed their bags. All that's missing is the gravestone marking the years of the union.

The Leo usually is vocal, so the Scorpio generally will know what's coming, what's on their mind, what annoys them, and so on. In contrast, the Scorpio is a silent assassin, trained in emotional warfare. They may try to clear up misunderstandings and communicate, to a point. But when a line has been crossed, they are out and nothing will bring them back. This behavior disturbs the Leo beyond belief, as they protest that they didn't see it coming—but they did, and they simply chose to ignore the warning signs. They tell their friends and followers that they thought their Scorpio was merely having a quiet day, week, month, or year, but that *is* the warning sign: first comes the deathly silence, as the Scorpio leaves the Leo emotionally and then, eventually, also physically. And if they ever hear that the Leo has been discussing them outside the sanctity of a therapist's couch (the Leo will need a Jungian therapist in this union), the Leo may have to ready themselves for a revenge attack. It may take a whole lifetime, but it's coming.

Even when they stay, the Scorpio will hold a pin at the ready to pop the ballooning ego of their lion, which may help the Leo grow but will be far from comfortable. For their part, the Scorpio must constantly review their motivation because karma is swift. With that power, as an agent of change, they must have honorable motives driving their actions or the universe will make moves to shut them down at some point, removing all potential for harming others and rendering them powerless—a fate worse than death for scorpions.

LOVE AND RESPECT

Evolved lions and scorpions are the most devoted and loyal of all the signs, which makes them fall in love on a whole other level. It's so comforting. Leo, in its flow, is the noblest of the signs, having integrity and a sense of loyalty that is awe-inspiring. They do not suffer fools, games, or disrespect, and if they look into the eyes of Scorpio and see the same moral compass and innermost desires, they will make the union work. When lions give their hearts, it's as if the sun walks by your side every day of your life. Equally, when a Scorpio sees their devotion, strength, and power matched, they will offer an empathy and respect that tames and melts the heart of even the fiercest lion. Sex is one thing, but naked love married to admiration and loving-kindness blows the mind of the cool-headed Scorpio.

REACHING NIRVANA

For this love match to endure, honesty must prevail. The Scorpio must be brave enough to confront the Leo about any less-than-appetizing behavior with empathy (no sign has more of that than a Scorpio) and communication. If the Leo has a quick temper or loose tongue, they will kill this love and its potential—and maybe even each other. They must try to use creative ways of self-expression, such as art, music, poetry, and sensuality. Understanding each other will take time. The Leo must learn how to be still and read situations calmly. The Scorpio must progress from their basic tit-for-tat mentality, in both love and life. When both forgive and match the other's devotion, all is well. Loyalty will keep these two together. Breaking trust isn't an option.

Taking refuge in a higher vision is preferable so that they may elevate their consciousness and make a positive impact in this life. Meditation, prayer, and forms of healing communication will help this couple grow and stay together.

If you are a Leo who loves a Scorpio, contemplate the following:

✧ Do you listen to your lover? Are you able to gauge their emotions?

✧ Are you emotionally intelligent? If not, ask your lover to help you learn.

✧ What does pride mean to you? How often does it hide behind your words or reactions?

✧ Do you believe in reincarnation? What does that mean for you and this relationship?

If you are a Scorpio who loves a Leo, contemplate the following:

✧ Does your lover trigger your empathy? Are you patient with them?

✧ When you feel loved, how does this change you? Now consider offering love without expectation, and sit with that.

✧ Do you suffer with attachment issues? If yes, try contemplating impermanence. Write down at least one or two examples or revelations daily for a week, and see how those changes begin to take root within your psyche. You will soon realize what matters and what really doesn't.

Leo–Pisces

RULED BY THE SUN AND JUPITER/NEPTUNE

Picture a strong, beautiful lion casually toying with a fish, which flutters in and out of its claws as the Leo ponders whether to eat it whole or throw it back in the river. Then comes the twist: the fish opens its deceptively large mouth to reveal rows of deadly teeth that snap shut on the lion's paws. The lion gives out an almighty roar and yanks back its paws, giving the fish its prized freedom, and it swims off. The moral of the story is that Pisces are not just submissive, martyr types, so don't underestimate them. It may take them longer to react than a short-fused lion, but they do snap back when threatened. And even though the Leo is the ruler of the jungle, they hold no authority over the oceans. Nobody rules over Pisces, not even Neptune. This fish will only be caught if, or when, it feels like it, and even then, it always has the option of slipping out of any net and disappearing into the vastness of the ocean. They need peace!

That said, a Leo is utterly spellbound by the magnificent being, shining with ethereal wisdom, that is a Pisces. A Pisces in its flow exists humbly, like a true artisan, and is the epitome of grace, gentle and strong and prepared to give a Leo the sincere adoration and admiration this cat needs—but only if they are given plenty of space to retreat and "do them" as well.

This union, when it works well, is marvelous. The Leo is majestic and regal, which gives them an air of cool detachment that the Pisces finds compelling and also complementary to their own style of living and loving. An oversharing, self-obsessed, and insecure cat is not the true manifestation of a Leo, so erase that from your mind; they are the imposters to the throne.

BOUNDARIES

Fish are on Earth to share their star-sent imagination, creativity, art, and sensitive healing ability with us all, but their sole purpose involves comprehending boundaries, just like their opposite sign, Virgo, although the latter has far too many and is prone to being rigid. Fish often lack consistency and staying power, but this can be overridden by an earth Moon, rising sign, or other major planet in their natal charts. Earthy fish are better placed to create a steady life brimming with depth and meaning. They need routine and structure to accomplish this, which a Leo can help them achieve.

A Leo usually has mastered the boundaries, but it also must encompass compassion and kindness, or they could develop superiority and annoyance toward the fish, which results in hurt feelings for both.

REACHING NIRVANA

I have dear friends born under the signs of Leo and Pisces who have been happily married for many moons. The secret seems to be compassionate love, yet the lion has very strong boundaries that keep the Pisces not only in check but swooning. Fish need real everything, and that includes love. And even if lions lack in other areas, when they give their heart to a lover, it's real.

With all unions, a belief in something more than one single existence is helpful. It pushes both to look beyond immediate satisfaction and more toward a long-term future. Working out together grounds these two, serving a noble charitable cause gives them a purpose bigger than the partnership, and exploring the natural terrain of the seas as divers or sailors or venturing into jungles together can provide adventure that keeps the relationship fresh and exciting.

If you are a Leo who loves a Pisces, contemplate the following:

✧ Do you ever adopt a superior attitude? If so, try empathy and compassion instead.

✧ What do you love about your partner? Always keep the list in mind.

✧ Do you go off on adventures together? If so, great! If not, plan some.

✧ Does your lover's sensitivity annoy you? If so, why?

If you are a Pisces who loves a Leo, contemplate the following:

✧ Do you ever play the victim?

✧ Are you ever slippery or dishonest? If so, work on that. If not, good job.

✧ Do you have interests outside the union? If not, make time for some. If yes, keep it up!

✧ Do you meditate? If not, learn, because this will help you attune to your intuition and higher mind.

Fire and Earth Signs Combined
Aries–Taurus
RULED BY MARS AND VENUS/GAIA

A ram and a bull generally are content to live in the same grassy field and share all that Mother Nature has to offer. Except that, as easygoing as a Taurus likes to think they are, they don't like to share. They would prefer if the Aries got their own field and maybe visited on weekends. For the sake of love, they will acquiesce—until the ram goes too far or tries to push the bull into changing. The ram will try with all its might and sass to shove the bull, or make calculations that ensure they get their own way, but the amused bull carries on chomping and is not swayed to budge even an inch, which pushes the Aries to the edge of their sanity. This kind of scenario regularly plays out for rams and bulls, even though it's a useless endeavor. The ram gets momentarily frustrated that it cannot have its way but will continue this maddening dance throughout eternity, such is the karma that brought them together. This also holds if a person has a Taurus Moon, Mars, or rising sign (maybe another planet, too) in their natal chart. You cannot push them into doing anything they don't want to do. And even if the Aries manages to gain one small win for the sake of compromise, resentment and opposition often are simmering beneath the surface of the bull's fair face.

Did I mention that Tauruses are usually rather gorgeous, being ruled by Venus? If a person has a Taurus Mars, they have an attractive, even beautiful, energy. A rising sign usually awards them with a face that glows with the light of Venus.

These two can love each other in ways that serve both partners and their higher selves, but acceptance without criticism or manipulation always must be present.

JOINED ENTERPRISE

An Aries is a dynamic firecracker who gets stuff done, often against the odds. A Taurus gets stuff done, too, but it takes a lot longer and is far less urgent.

The tendency for an Aries to be pushy is chilled by a Taurus Moon, rising sign, or Venus or Mars in their natal chart. In this case, the relationship has every chance of becoming an awesome one where give and take in equal measure can (and must) be had. The ram can't help being demanding or bossy, and if they are not take-charge types, that means they have a Pisces Moon or Mars or rising sign to chill them out.

An Aries is exciting by nature, and bulls love that about them.

A Taurus is extremely innovative in ways that defy the conventional interpretation of "creative," and an Aries knows a good idea when they see one. When the two team up, they can achieve a lot. An Aries is enterprising and can transform ideas into opportunities, and bulls appreciate this greatly. They see straight to their lover's pure heart and will stand by them long after the Aries has burned down all other bridges.

A Taurus and an Aries have the potential to build a marvelous life together, when the bull occasionally stands down and the ram realizes that two perspectives and points of view are better than one.

A Taurus is usually smitten with their dynamo and may secretly fear that the Aries will become bored, which won't happen if the bull remains strong in their own sense of self yet open to making sacrifices for the sake of compromise and the relationship.

For an Aries, the flame of romance burns bright and fast but rarely lasts—until they meet a Taurus, that is, who charms them with their pragmatic, resourceful approach to love and life. They may fail to demonstrate grand gestures, but when they love, they do so wholeheartedly. For them, it's all about humble, intimate shows of affection. For that, an Aries will remain yoked to a Taurus for all eternity, and in return, the bull will provide the Aries with support, love, and encouragement that will make them feel safe enough to grow and achieve.

REACHING NIRVANA

Compassion and empathy for each other will help both grow into the kind of people they were destined to become. That means that the Aries needs to learn that the Taurus is a fixed sign and usually cannot, or will not, be controlled. They also see right through attempts to control and coerce, so it's far wiser to plant seeds of suggestion and then patiently nurture them into bloom.

The Taurus needs to be patient with their fiery lover and avoid being stubborn as a form of rebellion. Honesty and communication are vital.

Healthy living, exercise, and compromise will help the two bond, as will consideration for each other. Meditation is helpful to both, as is self-awareness and acceptance without blame. Loving-kindness goes a long way.

The Taurus needs peace, routine, and stability, and the Aries likes to be out there, forging ahead. When each compromises their needs, they can achieve what they both need—a vegetable plot for the Taurus and a party room for the Aries.

If you are an Aries who loves a Taurus, contemplate the following:

✧ Do you push for your own way? If yes, consider how you may compromise.

✧ Are you calculating, based on your own ideas of how this union ought to be?

✧ Can you slow down and accept your magnificent self as well as your flaws?

✧ Do you criticize your lover? If yes, stop now. That builds resentments, which destabilize the foundations of your union. Try making positive suggestions instead.

✧ What makes you happy about this union?

If you are a Taurus who loves an Aries, contemplate the following:

✧ Are you able to compromise for your lover? What does this look like?

✧ Can you empathize with your ram?

✧ Do you have ideas that you could work on with your lover?

✧ Do you offer your lover your support?

Aries–Virgo
RULED BY MARS AND MERCURY/CHIRON

The ram and virgin are surprisingly well matched in many ways but obviously from completely different planets in others. Rams, unbeknownst to most, are refreshingly innocent and guileless and remain optimistic about life and humanity, regardless of age or harsh life experiences. Virgins find this endearing, especially because they, too, possess a youthful openness.

Of course, all of this is true only when the two are evolved (or evolving), in the positive flow of their signs, and haven't allowed disappointment to harden their hearts or cynicism to take root.

Their combined chemistry may well simmer into something lovely, and if they give this relationship enough time, mutual respect will grow as both partners recognize a kindred spirit, another being who wishes for the whole of humanity to be as up front and direct in their communications as they are. Life would be so much easier! Usually there are no hidden agendas or secret battles for power, which makes the relationship harmonious and less challenging than any other they may have tried, and failed, to solidify.

STABILITY

An Aries may prefer something more exciting than their solid and simple Virgo but, if a ram is truly ready to settle down, they will greatly appreciate that stability. As for the Virgo, they delight in the courage of their ram and will support them and encourage them to achieve incredible things, without even a hint of jealousy.

Of course, both signs, if unevolved or just having a bad day, week, month, or life, may result in something entirely different. Many believe that rams are the strongest of the two, but the Virgo has the potential to completely overpower the Aries if they want. Not working in their flow, the Virgo is calculating, controlling, and critical, which, over time, may dim even the bright, sparkly ram into submission. If this is the case, the Aries must work on their self-esteem and empowerment, which will restore the balance.

REACHING NIRVANA

Virgins must learn to transform their need for perfection into acceptance and praise their fiery lover as much as they can. Any habit of criticism or nitpicking must be faced and overcome because this will erode the love that certainly was there.

Rams are required to own and then discuss their hurt feelings without blame or anger. Bottling up any issues is not the answer because that volcano will erupt, and hell hath no fury like a ram who doesn't feel cared for.

Health is of paramount importance to us all, as is purpose, but both are vital for a Virgo to be able to thrive and provide support in any partnership. A spiritual practice also will help these two transcend the issues they may face. Together, they can start to build a strong sense of faith in life, the universe, and whatever their perception of God may be.

If you are an Aries who loves a Virgo, contemplate the following:

✧ Do you appreciate and praise your Virgo?

✧ Do you ever feel criticized? If so, do you speak up?

✧ Is physical exercise part of your life? If yes, great! If not, try it for a few weeks and notice the change in your happiness levels.

If you are a Virgo who loves an Aries, contemplate the following:

✧ What do you love about your Aries? Do you tell them?

✧ Are you a perfectionist? If so, how does that play out? And how is that helpful or not?

✧ Have you ever tried to meditate or retreat from distraction? If yes, good. If not, try. See how these methods impact your lover, your loved ones, and you.

Aries–Capricorn
RULED BY MARS AND SATURN

The goat and ram will share the same pasture, as long as they have enough space to roam independently (goats often go farther afield) and aren't required to stand next to each other 24/7. Oh, and both will need to have been disbudded and dehorned, or they are likely to butt heads. However, they may also cocreate an effective pasture management system, meaning they develop a symbiotic relationship that is beneficial and possibly even lucrative.

Unless goats have a good helping of Aquarius or Sagittarius in their charts, they grow old before their time and rather serious about everything. But more than this, they focus on their own futures: the accumulation of security, success, and a fortuitous relationship that offers more than hugs.

Rams are equally driven to achieve greatness, but they don't have the time or patience to wait around for anything or anyone for long, although as they grow a little older, this will change. Goats also are prone to becoming more spontaneous as they mature, although they often have made their name or fortune by then and can afford to be more carefree. In that respect, this pairing can work very well when both partners are a little farther down the road.

If an Aries has a Capricorn Moon or another earth sign and planet in their full charts, that will tone down their impatience and cancel out the potential explosions and amateur dramatics.

SOCIABLE

Contrary to popular opinion, goats are not somber, solitary figures; they actually like socializing. Rams absolutely love it. They probably met each other at an event or party where, presumably, the ram had dazzled the goat with their wit, dynamism, and breezy intelligence. Goats will happily take the opportunity to let down their hair, and if they feel safe, or are among their peers, they can match the ram with banter that smacks of brilliance and a light, attractive energy.

Rams are mesmerized by the confidence and strength of the goat because both are traits they aspire to have. When goats feel respected, they will drop their guard and allow themselves to get swept along by the excitement rams have to offer. But although goats can seem to possess confidence and swagger, many of them are merely acting. Just like swans, they may seem unruffled on the surface, but underneath they are paddling like mad. In contrast, rams don't feel the need to calculate that way, so their confidence, although often misplaced, is very real.

REACHING NIRVANA

When a Capricorn is truly comfortable in their own skin, nothing can destabilize them, not even an Aries. When an Aries has developed in maturity, this union works well, and it works long term, too. When they don't feel controlled, an Aries can commit and be faithful, which is paramount to a goat, who cares too much what others think to accept infidelity, unless it's been agreed to.

Recognizing the unique contribution each brings to the union is important, and small gestures will help keep their hearts tender and affectionate and maybe even prevent competitiveness. If both can see how preoccupied they can be with themselves, they will work to grow and make the other happy.

When an Aries slows down and perhaps incorporates mindfulness, relaxation, and breathing techniques into their days, they can harmonize with their goat and their life. When they are in the moment, enjoying its culmination together, they can both do well.

If you are an Aries who loves a Capricorn, contemplate the following:

✧ Does your goat know how to have fun?

✧ Do you know when to get real?

✧ Are you able to take your lover's feelings, goals, and dreams into consideration? And they yours?

If you are a Capricorn who loves an Aries, contemplate the following:

✧ Are you able to balance the need for quiet time with excitement?

✧ Do you think your lover is selfish? If so, are you a little self-serving, too? It's often a reflection.

✧ Do you plan little surprises for your lover? If no, try.

Sagittarius–Taurus
RULED BY JUPITER AND VENUS/GAIA

These two delight in bringing equal measures of inspiration and pleasure (the former is gifted by Sagittarius and the latter, Taurus) into each other's very different worlds.

Archers fascinate bulls, regardless of age. They are often brilliant and always inquisitive, brightening all our days with their unique intelligence. For a Taurus, they are simply irresistible. Bulls want them, and their sparkle, in their predictable lives.

In return, a Taurus brings a calm stability to the table, and unless the bull has a troublesome planet in Gemini or Leo, they are honorable, discerning beings who pride themselves on their reliability and trustworthiness. Archers know they have struck gold in that respect and have chanced upon a trustworthy confidant. This works well for family associations because they are karmically stuck with each other and forced to work through their differences, but as far as a long-term love goes, it will take a lot of work for both. The archer must be in a place to really want a relationship. A Taurus is not the sign to date if you are into casual affairs. They only will remain if they see a future with their fiery lover.

Archers are generous and perhaps a bit frivolous, which is fine if it's their own to give. But bulls value money; they usually work hard for it, and they can be a tad miserly. They also like material comfort and can be momentarily bought, or appeased, by shiny objects—a fact that archers use to their advantage, especially when they have offended a Taurus. This is not to say that archers don't like money—they absolutely love it—they just don't have the same attachments to material objects (unless they have Cancer Moon/

rising sign/other water sign or planet or had a financially unstable childhood).

Archers are luckier than most, often landing on their feet and always attracting more than they need, except mainly with enlightening experiences rather than simply material gains.

STIMULATION

If the bull operates in a low vibe and is jealous or possessive, that won't work for the archer, no matter how good everything else is. Unless they are bound by family ties, an archer will be off at the first whiff of possessiveness or resentment.

An archer, like their fellow freedom fighter the Aquarius, has to feel that their intrinsic need for freedom and independence is recognized and respected. If a Taurus is evolved, they will not suffer at the hand of the green-eyed monster and will reward the archer with their trust and love. And archers *are* trustworthy, as long as they are stimulated and challenged.

A Sagittarius helps a Taurus open their mind to new possibilities, and the innate wisdom of the archer thrills the bull to the point of excitement. Well, almost. They are more prone to raise an eyebrow yet keep their hooves firmly stuck in the mud.

A Taurus offers physical stimulation and sensuality that an archer finds intoxicating, and there is perhaps no sign as loyal as the bull, which is a new and welcome experience for a Sagittarius.

The mutable archer and fixed bull combination is not likely to produce a gushy romance, but more like an earthly interplay between two contrasting friends or mighty opponents. If they ever do become opponents, the stubborn, bullish Taurus will constantly push the archer to the brink of no return, where they have no option but to unleash arrows of truth upon that tough Taurean pelt. A Taurus feels duty bound to point out the hypocrisy that makes up a Sagittarius and their changeable version of truth and integrity. So the dance continues with neither one nor the other emerging unscathed.

REACHING NIRVANA

To arouse the potential of this union, communication is key. An archer needs to be careful how they phrase harsh truths and check their timing (maybe after dinner), and a Taurus must leave behind the memories of past relationship failures, learn to trust, and operate with an open heart. A give-and-take is required. Balance will allow this partnership to thrive, as will the study of spirituality and the nature of impermanence, which will help the Taurus overcome their materialistic desires and curb the archer's incessant search for anything other than what they already have.

If you are a Sagittarius who loves a Taurus, contemplate the following:

✧ Are you patient with your lover?

✧ Are you faithful? If yes, that's a strong foundation for longevity because a Taurus requires fidelity. If not, ask yourself why.

✧ What do you love about your bull?

If you are a Taurus who loves a Sagittarius, contemplate the following:

✧ Are you a trusting person? If yes, brilliant. If not, why?

✧ Do you practice the law of gratitude?

✧ Do you appreciate your lover's contribution to your life?

Sagittarius–Virgo
RULED BY JUPITER AND MERCURY/CHIRON

This pairing works well if both the archer and the virgin are suitably educated and dazzlingly smart. As far as the Virgo is concerned, there is no excuse for anyone to be ignorant in today's age of information, which means that if the archer's (or anyone else's) opinions are only lightly backed up, the Virgo licks their lips and shoots back flames of naked truth that sear right through to the bone. Except with a Sagittarius, who has scorch-proof skin.

The attraction usually begins as a meeting of the minds and only flows into something physical if both judge the other to be of equal intelligence in the verbal-sparring arena. Although the Sagittarius is usually game for trying something intimate sooner, the Virgo is more likely to make them wait. Luckily, archers relish a challenge so they wait and woo, using whatever resources they have. This is all overruled if the archer has Cancer Moon or other water signs in their full natal charts, in which case they are more defensive and unlikely to have the strength of spirit or staying power to cut through the multitude of smart rebuttals sent courtesy of the Virgo. However, the Virgo is doubtless both delighted and bemused by the fact that their sharp tongue and cutting truths are not only ineffective in wounding the slick archer but also matched in equal measure. To the casual observer, especially a Cancer, Pisces, or Scorpio, this linguistic battle is brutal, but to the archer and virgin, it's foreplay. Finally, they have met their match: a lover who doesn't take offense easily or react with prideful anger. Even though the Virgo is unlikely to admit this, the archer recognizes the compatibility, is mesmerized, and becomes determined to hang up their bow and arrow and give this relationship a shot. The trouble is, archers get bored, can be emotionally lazy, and may stray, which is a total deal-breaker to virgins, who require total dedication and earnestness.

A Sagittarius is strongly opinionated but doesn't always research the facts, unless they have been burned publicly or are the academic type, but even these wise ones are predisposed to be lacking emotional intelligence and tact. A Virgo gets this on a profound level because they can be the same in the tactless department, although they are usually more prone to overanalyze and feel bad after all is said and done. Unlike their counterpart, they do worry about hurting others with their razor-sharp comments. They also prefer to research topics using several sources because they are afraid of being in the dark; they don't like the dark. A Sagittarius doesn't wait around to feel bad about anything (unless they have compassionate or emotional planets in their charts). As the more fearless, or feckless, sign, they welcome both light and dark if there is the potential to score in their game of life. Thrill and adventure are worth double points.

TRUTH SLAYERS

No other signs could truly hold the title "truth slayer," although a Sagittarius (like its opposite sign, Gemini) has been known to occasionally sidestep or bend the truth if it gets in the way of a good story or proves to be too personally inconvenient. A Virgo is usually very black and white in terms of their version of truth. But gray areas do exist, and just because some people may be more creative or economical with the truth doesn't mean they are liars. Try telling a Virgo that, though. They are uncompromising in that respect, and if they deem someone to be less than frank, they will dismiss their every word. If they ever do find themselves in a situation when they are required to be less than honest, perhaps to save someone's feelings, for example, they take themselves on a rollercoaster ride of justification. This is why the archer can be good for them, to help them laugh at themselves. That is just what they need.

Both signs, in their flow, are honest, logical, good people who have no interest in hurting or controlling anyone else. Virgos have a bad rep for micromanaging, but that control is usually only to do with their own environment and mainly due to their own fears and insecurities, which archers pierce through in fractions of seconds, rarely taking any notice, never mind offense.

Archers have an uncanny knack for spouting truth and wisdom and then quickly moving on to the next topic. A Virgo in their flow misses nothing, to the point of reviewing whole interactions in their heads, obsessively, long after it's all over. And that's the point: a Virgo must learn to let go of fear and be present in the moment, which counteracts the neurosis and anxiety with which untrained virgins are prone to suffer. And archers, well, they are the prophets, and so much of their wisdom is shot through them from the cosmos and rarely thought of again. For these reasons, both partners have so much to learn and gain from each other. The archer needs to become more mindful about what they say and when, and the Virgo needs to let go of the impulse to control an interaction and open their heart and mind to the present moment. That's all any of us ever really have.

REACHING NIRVANA
The archer soothes their Virgo into caring or worrying less about small inconsequentialities, encouraging them to instead embrace the freedom found in moving on and grasping the moment.

The Virgo eventually reveals their pure heart to the archer, who vows to care for and protect them for eternity. Neither is likely to have been labeled "sweet" by any other friend or lover, but that is just what these two are together. This pairing has the potential to extract the nectar, transforming sour lemons into a sugary lemonade that comforts both and results in a tranquil acceptance. With naked truth, patience, and loving-kindness, this match can play out for many lifetimes.

If you are a Sagittarius who loves a Virgo, contemplate the following:

✧ Do you see through your lover's harsh words to the softness of their core?

✧ Do you help your lover lighten up?

✧ Are you as truthful as they say? With yourself? With others?

If you are a Virgo who loves a Sagittarius, contemplate the following:

✧ Are you hard on your lover? On yourself? If yes, reflect on why, and try to be softer.

✧ Do you trust yourself?

✧ What are your biggest fears? Now consider that everything is impermanent and resist those fears.

Sagittarius–Capricorn
RULED BY JUPITER AND SATURN

When it comes to a union between the archer and the goat, you wrongly may assume that the archer will be the partner to come out on top, that they'll hit the old goat with their flame-tipped arrow or Cupid's bow, depending on their mood that day, and then hold up their hands, declaring themselves the winner. But goats are as tenacious as bulls. They're just a lot craftier and more reserved.

A Sagittarius doesn't have a crafty bone in their body; they are proud that what you see is what you get, and they wonder why everyone else can't be as honest, direct, and no-nonsense. It is, in fact, far more complex than that, especially if they have a Moon, Mars, or Venus in the neighboring sign of Scorpio; in that case, they *wish* they were that simple.

If the goat has fire sign planets in their charts, it'll be much easier for these two to form and sustain a union. This pairing is unlikely to begin as a meeting of higher minds—it's more base level and physical. There will be plenty of passion and, if they are compatible sexually (archers like it steamy), the archer will probably make more of an effort. But if they take their time, giving each other space (archer) and respect (goat), they have a chance to build something fabulous.

Neither is particularly creative by nature, so they are keen for inspiration. Archers *are* often brimming with the stuff. They have a verve and an ardor for life and gleefully embrace each new day, which is rejuvenating for the Capricorn, who gets off on this kind of bounce. Of course, there are archers who don't know how to tap into this energy at all, which is courtesy of their boss, Jupiter. They should go exploring or hiking with their goat, spending more time frolicking in nature, away from worldly concerns, maybe sitting still atop a mountain. That ought to do it.

The Capricorn, when not flowing well, can be a drain on one's chi, like an energy vampire (a trait they share with opposite sign Cancer and with Scorpio).

ASPIRATIONAL

This union brings to each what they really wish they naturally possessed themselves. The Capricorn is enthralled and slightly envious of the free-spirited, adventure-loving Sagittarius, and the archer, well, they like the strong morals they aspire to, and if they have a healthy dose of Capricorn in their charts, they are likely to hold standards that will match a goat's—although if they have a Gemini or Leo Moon, aspirational may be as far as they get. Either way, both are a long shot if they aren't committed to self-improvement and haven't realized how barren a busy life is. Unless, that is, they fall in love, they rejoice in each other's differences, and they invest in making each other happy.

REACHING NIRVANA

Both love to learn, and goats enjoy being the teacher. The archer's wisdom is more sporadic, with moments of prophecy laced throughout the mundane. Finding an authentic teacher and path to explore the workings of the mind will help them progress as students of life. Both may look for power over the other, so equality is important for these two to sidestep resentment and communicate with open hearts.

The fact is that they both have much to gain from the other, and although this partnership does have the potential to work out, it will take time and a whole heap of forbearance. Simple patience won't be enough. Kindness and compassion will enable them to recognize the vulnerability beneath a tough exterior, which will open a whole new level of understanding and true love.

If you are a Sagittarius who loves a Capricorn, contemplate the following:

✧ Do you share similar values? Think about it, and make a list. Maybe make it together.

✧ Are you able to blend your optimism with your goat's caution?

✧ Are you ready for this commitment? What does this look like to you?

If you are a Capricorn who loves a Sagittarius, contemplate the following:

✧ Are you prone to pessimism? Do you hide this behind your perception of reality? Think about this.

✧ Try being positive for half a day, and note how you feel.

✧ If you are not prone to pessimism, do you attract people who would benefit from this exercise? If so, share it with them.

✧ Do you spend time in nature? It's important for your well-being, so make it part of your routine and track the benefits.

Leo–Taurus

RULED BY THE SUN AND VENUS/GAIA

A majestic lion and an elegant bull. Surely, the lion would eat the bull for breakfast! This may happen in the wild, but make no mistake, this is an equal match of strength that has the potential to rouse passion and create a totally devoted love. If both are evolved, this love provides emotional and material nourishment and an ardor that both partners will treasure.

The Taurus is, generally, an incredible provider, and as long as the Leo is not too much of a taker, they will be content and appreciative, which means that the bull will have what they need most: to feel valued and prized.

Lions are proud. That goes for the quieter, more noble beasts as well as the showier types, who demand and command in equal measure—except that nobody smart would boss around a bull. If lions ever fail to recognize that, they surely will end up licking their wounds. They can launch the attack, but the Taurus will stand stoically until the lion physically tires. Then the bull will give a toss of their horns, and the lion is done for. If the Leo pushes one time too often to get their own way, there is no going back. That's why it's wise for the Leo to be careful and not take the bull's love or kindness for granted. The Leo is also generous to a fault and so open-hearted that they warm the hearts of even the coldest beings, but their need for recognition and praise can grate on the humble bull's nerves.

All of this sounds like hard work, right? With these two, it often is. Bulls relish challenges—in fact, they rise to them. Taming a lion may not have been on their to-do list, and they may moan about it or hesitate to accept the dare, but if they do, they are all-in and the Leo purrs in delight at the attention.

If the Taurus has a Leo Moon or rising sign and the Leo has a Taurus Moon or rising sign, this partnership may harmonize faster than I've described, but even then, there will be tension and friction until they have had a chance to test each other's boundaries and decide that they want to make it permanent.

ADMIRATION

Bulls value affection and sensuality, and lions crave admiration and attention, but along the way, they may manage to meet on neutral ground where both of their needs will be met. Until they attain their own version of neutral Switzerland, though, there may be constant struggle. The more the Leo demands, the more opposition and stubbornness they meet, and there are only so many times they can sort things out with kisses and caresses.

The Leo adores nothing more than a good argument that can then erupt into a passionate encounter, but bulls eventually tire of this dynamic, and they will pry their lion's claws away from their necks and head for the door to find some peace.

REACHING NIRVANA

Bulls and lions both can be materialistic, and this won't serve them well in any long-term association unless the money is endless and their assets continue to grow. Although Leos can be grandiose and extravagant, bulls are usually a tad shrewder with their resources, so this can be a bone of contention. Moderating their attachment to worldly gain will allow them to see who they really are, underneath it all, as will giving back and helping those less fortunate. With a higher purpose, these two can take on the world and make it a better place.

A regular meditation practice can help both out of mental ruts, too.

If you are a Leo who loves a Taurus, contemplate the following:

✧ Do you push your lover to get a reaction? If yes, why? Or is it the other way around?

✧ List the good things about this relationship.

✧ Do you require a lot of praise and recognition? If so, do you know how superficial this is? Your soul gives you all of this and more, if you take the time to listen.

If you are a Taurus who loves a Leo, contemplate the following:

✧ Do you see past your lion's arrogance to their warm and open heart?

✧ Does your Leo make everything seem more beautiful? Do you tell them that?

✧ If your lover needs constant praise and recognition, can you try to help them see that needing less of it would be better for them?

✧ Are you stubborn with your lover or ever resentful? If so, why? And when?

Leo–Virgo
RULED BY THE SUN AND MERCURY/CHIRON

Leo and Virgo are next to each other on the zodiac wheel; Leo comes first (of course!) and then the virgin, who is ready to serve the monarch. Well, up to a point. If this union lasts longer than a Super Bowl ad, rules will need to be established. Although the Leo will attempt to choose those rules, the Virgo is not easily controlled by anyone for long, no matter how much they may love them.

The Leo may try to use their feline charms and cunning on the Virgo, but it won't wash in the long run. The Virgo is as brilliant as Sirius, the brightest star, and what they may lack in cunning they more than make up for with perceptiveness. If the Leo realizes this, and if the Virgo sees through all the lion's tricks and decides to stay anyway, the magic can begin.

Mercury and Venus are like the Sun's entourage, and in any natal chart, they never will be more than two signs away. These two may seem as if they are from different galaxies, and they will need to have one of the other's planets to form common ground. Luckily, they almost certainly do. It's more likely than not that the Leo has planets in Virgo and that the Virgo has a Moon or at least one other planet in Leo, which means they are able to get each other on various levels: mental (Mercury connections), physical (Mars), spiritual (Moon, Saturn, and North Nodes), or possibly all three. If so, together they can weather any storm life sends them.

If they don't have matching planets or a rising sign, it's unlikely that either will tolerate the other's flaws for long, no matter how blinding Leo's light may be. The Leo is, or believes they are, descended from royalty, and if a lover takes more than they offer, or has a self-absorption that rivals their own, it's usually off to the guillotine.

Luckily for the lion, the Virgo is all about service and giving generously, but if the Leo is crass, vulgar, or too vain, the good times will soon fade. A Leo loves drama and attention, and, if they feel they have been wronged or their pride wounded, they will drag their virgin into all sorts of battles. Eventually, the Virgo will get wise or exhausted, critical, and even cruel. The Leo is far better off preventing this by consciously working with heart over ego.

STARS ALIGN

When both partners are evolved, the Leo becomes protective of their virgin, regardless of who has the more masculine or feminine energy. They manage to see what most past lovers have not: Virgo's true, shining honesty and pure radiance. A virgin's love can make any other fade into insignificance. If the Leo is not evolved, though, it's simply a facade, and eventually the virgin will see through the Leo's apparent selflessness and realize how scheming they are, which quite literally breaks their heart.

No partner can heal the other's wounds quite like these two, which is why both need to tread carefully and respectfully, holding the law of karma close at all times: what we reap, so shall we sow.

The Leo is the clever cat who will go all-out to win over the virgin. The Leo also is the cool cat, who is not the easiest to win over at all. But when they feel smitten, they open their heart, life, and bank account—the latter being the most important declaration of love, as far as virgins are concerned. If the Virgo feels that the Leo is too selfish, though, that must be addressed lovingly and quickly; otherwise, the virgin will begin to criticize or belittle the lion, or neglect them to the point that they roar with indignance, and then all sorts of rivalry and meanness can arise as they set out to gain power over each other.

Good communication and open hearts are key for these two, as is self-awareness.

REACHING NIRVANA

Virgos are prone to excessive nervous mental energy, and they are hesitant to trust. If they have been hurt badly or betrayed in the past, the Leo has their work cut out for them and must be patient, kind, and generous.

If the Leo suffers from deep-seated insecurities and acts in strange ways to compensate for this, the Virgo may be able to help them become confident in a more authentic way, while the Leo helps the Virgo laugh and feel joy. If we take the bigger picture into consideration, it is unwise to expect any other person to heal us or make us feel better long term; only we can do that with faith in a higher wisdom, being, or universal energy. When you know that this life is only one of many, it grows your confidence, reducing the urge to grasp at things that don't really matter.

Meditation is valuable for us all, but for the Virgo, this type of mind training is immensely beneficial. If the Leo and Virgo can, as a couple, partake in it as part of a joint routine, their attachments will be healthy, allowing love and trust to flourish.

If you are a Leo who loves a Virgo, contemplate the following:

✧ Do you give as much as you receive?

✧ What do you love about your Virgo? List the reasons.

✧ Are you prone to being a tad self-absorbed?

If you are a Virgo who loves a Leo, contemplate the following:

✧ Do you laugh together? Remember, it's important not to take life too seriously.

✧ Are you an anxious person? If so, have you tried to meditate?

✧ Is this union balanced? Think about it, and make moves to rectify things if it isn't; otherwise, this will cause you issues later.

Leo–Capricorn
RULED BY THE SUN AND SATURN

The goat and lion meet and live happily ever after. That's how it should read, and that is usually how it goes. To them, it feels like a heavenly match (for the Leo at least; the Capricorn is usually more interested in how the match will play out here on Earth) because they have so much in common. However, a whole heap of work and practical negotiation about exactly how this union is going to play out is required. Doesn't sound very romantic, does it? But to both of them, pragmatically planning a future is as romantic as it gets and must take the needs of both into consideration.

The Leo brings more sunshine, fun, and lightness to the shaded world of the Capricorn (unless the Capricorn has a Leo Moon or other sunny planets themselves).

The Capricorn brings respect, status, and the discipline that Leo often lacks. The lion also needs to feel proud of their partner, and Capricorns have the sort of achievements that will impress their Leo.

When they team up, they are able to galvanize each other's might, influencing others and the world. But for these two to survive, there ought to be a common cause or theme driving them forward. It can't just be having kids; it needs to be living an altruistically based life, rather than simply raising a few more lions or goats in their own likeness. The Leo requires a more significant stage than a living room, even if that room is in a plush, stately home. They both need a big picture to remain committed to anyone. That said, they likely will have children because both are concerned with legacy, even if they are not aware of it.

The Capricorn is usually ambitious, and they can be snobbish, too. If their partner doesn't have a crown, power, class, money, or social standing, they will need to be famous, have the ability to make them look good in some way, or have apodictic *potential* for greatness at the very least. The Leo is shiny enough, and if they end up in the public eye because of who their lover is, all the better.

There may be struggles for dominance when push comes to

shove. Unless Leo has a Capricorn Moon, Mars, or rising sign, the goat will be in control for most of the time.

SHINY SOULS

On a superficial level, the reason this pairing can work well is due to the fact that the Capricorn is extremely concerned with how they are perceived through the public lens (even if they are not famous). Being perceived as successful is often as important to them as actually being successful. So having a shiny, gorgeous, Sun-ruled Leo on their arm is very much a part of that.

This pairing often works best if the Leo is the center of attention when they first meet (or if it's decided that this will be how things play out) and Capricorn is the one keeping the boat afloat, plotting their course and offering sage advice. The Capricorn would, perhaps, need to provide financial support as well as astute and intelligent strategies on who should assume which role, what the common goal is, and how they are going to achieve it.

If the lion is a strong and noble version of themselves, they will be concerned with a higher cause, such as fighting injustice or defending those in need, and are often inspired by their Capricorn to go that much further. If they don't have that higher purpose, many just end up bobbing along.

REACHING NIRVANA

Both goats and lions are prone to being selfish. It all comes back to the same low-vibe issue if they are not trying to be better humans. I will say it once more: for these two to form a lasting partnership and survive the storms of distraction and inertia, it's imperative that they have a higher vision at heart, a belief that takes them out of themselves and their own short-term needs. For this reason, exploring spirituality, until they find a version that sticks, is the best way to achieve an enduring love. Giving themselves to genuine causes that serve humanity but also will end up serving them in the long run is beneficial as well.

If you are a Leo who loves a Capricorn, contemplate the following:

✧ Do you aspire to make a positive contribution to the world?

✧ What do you love about your goat? Do you respect them?

✧ Are you able to give and receive love in this union?

If you are a Capricorn who loves a Leo, contemplate the following:

✧ What initially attracted you to your lover?

✧ Do you support your lion, helping them reach their goals, or is it the other way around?

✧ Are you generous with your love and affection?

✧ Do you respect your partner? Define this.

Fire and Air Signs Combined

Aries–Gemini

RULED BY MARS AND MERCURY

A ram and twins galloping across fields and chasing each other through meadows is how best to picture these two signs together. They bring out the childlike innocence and purity of spirit in each other, and this may happen at any stage of their lives. They are so happy to have found a lover who has equal amounts of energy *and* an infectious passion for life. Whereas these two likely have exhausted past lovers with their high-octane cavorting, they are unlikely to do that this time around. The only concern the heavens may have for them is that they could push each other to the extreme, to the limits of human capability, because neither knows how to apply the brakes in anything that they do. They must learn how to do this, or they will burn out.

Mars-ruled rams have physical meltdowns, however that manifests, and Mercury-ruled Gemini have mental implosions—it all can be rather dangerous, even violent. Gemini (and those with Gemini rising, Moon, or Mercury signs) are known as gas bags and for good reason: if you go near them with an open flame, and that's just what an Aries is, you are likely to be blown up. So although this has all the makings of a successful union, it also has the potential to burn down the house, block, or entire village.

An Aries will do very well in life when they consciously adopt the same goal their opposite sign, Libra, is subconsciously striving for: balance. Gemini, like their opposite sign, Sagittarius, is also on a lifelong quest to learn moderation. If they both succeed, the stars will shine for them.

Unevolved, the Gemini is ignorant, and they wrongly assume they are a skilled communicator just because they can talk the paint off a wall, but the truth is that the paint just wants to escape. A Gemini, not working in their flow, only listens to half of a story or instruction and forgets it a millisecond later because they have become so excited that they will almost burst if they don't share their joke, funny story, or latest gossip. Talking is good, but listening is best, and when you've mastered the art of talking less and listening and studying more, that is true communication, which is what the Gemini is duty bound to master.

RIVALRY

A Gemini may get fed up with being bossed around by an Aries, but they are going to have to accept that this is unlikely to change. Rams feel justified to take over because if they left it to the Gemini, things would take too long to actualize. Aries is a cardinal (leadership) sign, and they are mutable, which means they are constantly changing—their minds, their interests, their partners—until they meet the Gemini, that is, and their game is finally equally matched by a worthy partner.

It's impossible to get bored with rams; they are excitement personified. So twins often will put up with being told what to do and when to do it. An Aries competes with their own shadow. They love to help other people but only if they don't do better than the Aries, and even then, the Aries will have difficulty accepting that.

The Aries can be jealous, which fuels them to be even more competitive, and so the cycle begins. It's not the simmering slow-burning envy of a Scorpio or a Taurus; it's just a quick flash of unpleasantness. So the Gemini must rein in their flirtatious ways and ask themselves if they would be happy to accept this behavior from their lover. Unlikely! They, too, can be a little possessive if they have a Scorpio/Taurus/Leo rising. With a Mars or Moon sign, that potential is tripled.

REACHING NIRVANA
An Aries is honest, and a Gemini *will* get there, but it may take a little more persuasion. Living in their own truth is far more important and aligns them with their higher selves. Both partners need to tap into their intuition or higher minds, which can only be accessed by sitting still and being quiet. If they manage to do this, perhaps with regular meditation or prayer, they will achieve balance and moderation, which will lead to a love that grows and endures.

If you are an Aries who loves a Gemini, contemplate the following:

✧ Do you boss around your lover? If so, can you try not to? Maybe make suggestions instead and ask your lover to tell you when they feel bossed about.

✧ Is the passion still alive? What do you do to help keep the flame burning?

✧ Is your life balanced? If not, make notes as to why, and make a pact to try harder.

✧ Are you living in your own truth? What does that mean for you?

If you are a Gemini who loves an Aries, contemplate the following:

✧ Does your lover excite you?

✧ What does moderation mean to you?

✧ Do you know how to both listen and speak?

✧ Do you read? Knowledge feeds your soul.

✧ Do you have spiritual beliefs? What are they?

Aries–Libra
RULED BY MARS AND VENUS

Opposites attract and react, and the rest is history. Either that or it's a chemistry experiment, carried out for observational purposes only, that produces world-changing results or blows up the lab. Aries is a fire sign, after all, and no amount of Libra in their full charts will take that away.

For these two to want to form a union, it's likely that the Libra has Aries or another fiery planet in that karmic wheel known as the natal chart, and for the Aries to have enough patience to handle the dillydallying of Libra, they, too, must have some other gracious planet going on somewhere (like a Libra rising sign or Moon or maybe Taurus or even Cancer). The point is, if you are reading this, you have far more impacting your personality than just your Aries or Libra Sun sign; otherwise, you wouldn't even want to read this sign combination because the relationship wouldn't have lasted past one annoying date. There is unlikely to be any middle ground here, which is strange because Libra is all about the middle way. They require balance, harmony, and cooperation, just like rams need and attract a good challenge.

MUTUAL RESPECT

This relationship holds the potential to help both parties grow and heal from past pain. It also triggers a mutual understanding, respect, and compassion. The scales accommodate the ram's need for space and freedom of expression, however that manifests, and a tranquil and nonjudgmental space is ideal for an Aries to grow.

A Libra will allow an Aries to vent, patiently encouraging them and standing by them as they work through both major and minor issues. An Aries appreciates this support and the logical and fair mind of their lover, which brings a sense of peace and harmony that they may not have found with any other. They do not feel judged (unless the Libra is the darker side of the sign), and they feel safe to be open and brutally honest. A Libra helps them see both sides of an often one-sided version of truth or reality.

REACHING NIRVANA

An Aries can get so caught up in themselves that they forget the enormous contribution their Libra brings. Taking time to show their Libra that they are loved is important, and it only needs to be something simple, such as a candlelit home-cooked dinner, because small gestures of affection go a long way.

An unevolved ram only values financial and tangible offerings, but this partnership offers far more blessings than that. Emotional support, tolerance, and understanding are far more beneficial on a soul level than anything money can buy. That said, all things need to be balanced so one can support the other long term.

Working on the law of gratitude is important for both, as are regular meetings to discuss areas that need to be adjusted to acquire equilibrium.

If you are an Aries who loves a Libra, contemplate the following:

✧ What unique contributions does your lover bring to your life? List them.

✧ Do you listen to your lover and value their advice?

✧ What annoys you? Can you find solutions to address this, without blame or criticism?

✧ What do you love about your Libra?

If you are a Libra who loves an Aries, contemplate the following:

✧ Does your ram inspire you? If so, how?

✧ Is this relationship balanced? If so, great. If not, what changes can you make to address this?

✧ Do you give without expectation?

✧ List the reasons why you love your ram.

Aries–Aquarius
RULED BY MARS AND SATURN/URANUS

This is not considered a match made in heaven. It's more like an intergalactic roller-coaster ride. Or think of it like a movie trilogy, with these two spinning through space and time, the saga spanning lifetimes. As the movie stretches on, both parties simply want to reach a satisfying end that never arrives. Still, they have a magnetic draw, delighting in the energy and chemistry that sizzled when they first met.

It's hard not to notice these two in a crowd, yet they rarely feel the need to compete with each other, unless it's to measure the levels of patience they each have, which is zero. They hold a mutual respect; they recognize that they bring complementary skills and blessings to the table; and they know that when they're getting along, the world is indeed their oyster.

An Aries and an Aquarius are undeniably fascinated with each other (unless one or both have a conformist Libra or ambitious Capricorn and Taurus Moon, a rising sign, or other planets). Both are equally unpredictable and unrestrained, with little regard for social constraints or the opinions of others, and this bodes well for a long-lasting union full of zest and verve, even if it's challenging and uncomfortable at times.

There is an underlying tension for an Aries that makes it hard to settle down into a routine with an Aquarius. An Aries is high maintenance and needs frequent stimulation, which an Aquarius provides naturally, consistently, and effortlessly. This kind of union would make a Virgo or Cancer wince, but it can work for these two, if both are comfortable with constant change and expectations are adjusted amicably when required.

SACRED CONTRACTS

An Aries and an Aquarius have strong karmic connections and willingly come to each other's aid without reason or delay. Even if the union ends, they often will remain friends for life; neither holds a grudge because they are too busy marching onward. Both forgive readily and are baffled by folks who hold ill will toward someone they once professed to love. They have usually fought on the same side in many battles over the course of multiple incarnations, which evokes a loyalty that transcends the mundane and defies logic. In fact, both will accept behavior from the other that other signs would find insane because they each know that life is a school and that learning through experience and trial and error ensures a soul reward.

The two are often unconsciously linked to each other's journey of spiritual growth and discovery, and for this reason, they have plenty to learn as a couple, or even as friends. Their relationship is indeed a higher love that is uncomplicated in that respect. They adore each other on a spiritual level that needs no roots in a worldly love, which is too often riddled with expectation, conditions, and rules. Neither sign asserts ownership over the other, which gives this union a fighting chance of becoming a forever love.

Both an Aries and an Aquarius are lit up by anything new and exciting and have a thirst for adventure, which keeps them on their toes. Here's the problem, though: an Aries is ruled by Mars and is driven by passion, lust, and fire, whereas an Aquarius is cool-headed and only ever dips into that unbridled passion momentarily. This often leaves the Aries with a hunger for more, addicted to those fleeting moments when they felt that they had the full attention of their Aquarius. An Aries jumps into the union with both feet, and although an Aquarius is loyal to the end and will defend their Aries until their last breath, they are never *fully in*. As their Aquarius remains both attached and detached, the Aries becomes increasingly frustrated. This can lead to acting out for attention or attempting to make their Aquarius jealous, which rarely works with a water bearer, who is the embodiment of cool rationale.

The Aquarius has an acute understanding of their Aries's irrational behavior and will work intellectually to soothe their fears, but an Aries will never be able to get 100 percent comfortable in this union, nor will they solely "own" their partner. The minute an Aquarius feels that an Aries is trying to control them, they step on the brakes and resist or simply rebel. This is not contrived, nor is it a manipulative attempt to keep the Aries interested; it just is what it is. As a result, the Aries remains caught in the net, unless they choose to move on to someone who will indulge them in that respect.

REACHING NIRVANA

When an Aries and an Aquarius are in love, all previous experiences and rules may as well be discarded. There is no framework that these two can follow easily; they have to patiently carve out their own. Patience doesn't come naturally to either, but luckily, the laughter stays close to the surface. Any tantrum, anger, excessive emotion, or attempt to control will leave the Aries standing alone with cosmic dust in their face. Instead, speaking honestly and openly is the best way to evoke compassion from an Aquarian. For this union to become enduring love, communication is vital. This is true of all signs, but an Aries must not expect too much change from an Aquarius, or they will be disappointed. Instead, they must request specifically what they need because although the Aquarius is an intuitive and advanced soul, their awareness and empathy are usually reserved for humanity as a whole and simple issues need to be spelled out for them. If you are the Aries, don't play games; just speak your truth gently and own your feelings without blame. How you feel is never another person's fault, so examine your own reaction.

Both are progressive signs, so this union respects their need for independence and their ability to give each other the space they crave. It only works if both partners are confident in their own sense of self, though. Otherwise, the relationship may draw out the needy and insecure five-year-old who resides inside all of us. If the Aries wants to persist, they will need to learn to enjoy the freedom they are given, which comes from a place of respect, not indifference, and to leave the door open for their Aquarian lover. Then both may enjoy plenty of freedom to build their confidence with the knowledge that they are safe, loved, and trusted.

Both signs love a cause that serves humanity, and both believe in a higher purpose, so working on something inspiring together is a good way to bond past the passion and work through issues, as and when they arise.

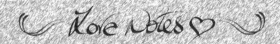

If you are an Aries who loves an Aquarius, contemplate the following:

✧ Do you feel like you have met your wave maker before, in some other life?

✧ Was the attraction instant? Is that attraction still present?

✧ Are you able to team up and work on a noble cause that helps more vulnerable beings?

✧ Does your lover excite you with their unpredictable nature, or does it annoy you? Was this always the case? If not, what changed?

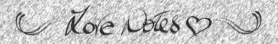

If you are an Aquarius who loves an Aries, contemplate the following:

✧ Does your Aries excite you? How so?

✧ Do you recognize and respect their values?

✧ Are you both honest with each other?

✧ Can you relax together? Do you get out in nature?

Leo–Gemini

RULED BY THE SUN AND MERCURY

The lion and the twin are a fabulous match. They are both young at heart, no matter their age, and have a light yet strong and extremely loving relationship. If the Leo is utterly devoted, the Gemini is content, and vice versa.

Problems can arise if the Gemini's roving eye takes over, or the Leo feels a lack of affection. Then, either one of them may walk out or explore the multitude of other options that are, no doubt, on offer. If the Leo has a mind to cheat, they are usually honest as to why and what the Gemini did to cause them to stray. (It's always someone else's fault.) If that happens, the breezy air sign will detach like an iceberg calving from the edge of a melting glacier.

Often, though, this pairing has the ability to work through any issues they may have with patience and humor. If kids are involved, they usually do stay together.

A Leo in full flow is the most gracious cat on earth and readily supports their Gemini in all of their endeavors with a kindness and love that boosts the twin's well-being and confidence. In return, the Gemini in full flow is contemplative and discerning, offering the Leo sage advice that comes from a considerate position. If either or both have water signs in their charts (Moon/rising/Mercury, etc.), this will give them a sensitivity that can be touching and heartfelt. Or if they are prone to settle in the realms of lower ego, they can become defensive, taking everything as a slight and becoming too quick to pounce.

Both give stalwart and inspired advice, although the twin doesn't feel the need to remind everyone, at every given moment, about all the successful moves that have been made based on that advice. The Leo is often the antithesis of this, which results in the Gemini's refusal to ask for any guidance or else to do the opposite of what the Leo suggested, simply to avoid the crowing.

No matter what, lions and twins always leave a mark wherever they go, good, bad, or ugly. When they combine all that airy aptitude for brilliance with the dynamism and passion of fire, it works to provide a constant source of fascination and interest that binds them for life—or leads them to become bitter enemies. Both can hold grudges, and don't let either of them tell you any different.

When the Gemini hurts the Leo, the lion will roar and fight loudly and then slink off to lick their paws and quietly growl if the perpetrator's name is mentioned or an associated memory is aroused, perhaps even years later.

But the Gemini has a different recipe for vengeance. We are not talking about revenge in the Scorpio sense; it's far more subtle than that. Remember, they are the messengers of the zodiac, and that can work well or not so well, depending on the individual. A few whispered words in just the right ears can cause plenty of trouble, planting seeds of doubt where they may impact the lion the most—mainly anything that can hurt their prideful ego, and with an ego that big, it's not too hard to do.

HEART-OPENERS

Most of the time the Leo needs to feel that they are *better* than their peers. This results from a distant soul memory of being an ungracious royal. If they see themselves as the more intelligent, wealthier, the more beautiful, etc., it's only then that the person standing next to them will be allowed to share their stage. But the moment they feel that someone is all of the above and maybe more, they become cranky and competitive.

The Gemini can be a little like that, too. They keep moving so they don't have to face themselves. They spin yarns to themselves and whoever will listen and do all they can to sidestep responsibility and reality. When they team up with a lion, both have the capacity to open their hearts to each other. Why? Because they both secretly suffer from imposter syndrome, unhappily comparing their lives with everyone else. So their mutual sympathy endures, and it may even help them climb out of the gladiator's pit of rivalry and illusion.

REACHING NIRVANA

The evolved lion and Gemini are cool individually, and even cooler as a couple. They stand tall in their light and generously shine it on others who may need some sunshine and sparky intelligence, without the need to feel superior. The twins are the sharpest tools in the zodiacal box of tricks, so when these two combine as a force for good, the only way to describe the union is *magnanimous*.

Lower ego and pride should not be allowed to hold them back, so any work they can do in this area, to become more aware, will help them in the long term. Humor is a necessary tool because the Gemini will tell the Leo the ugly truth and then make them laugh, and vice versa. Faith in a higher vision helps us all, but in the case of these two, it will enable them to rise above the worldly chatter and find their version of God.

If you are a Leo who loves a Gemini, contemplate the following:

✧ What do you appreciate about this relationship?

✧ Do you love without expectation?

✧ Do you demand recognition for any advice you gave and your lover used? Why?

✧ What is your interpretation of love?

If you are a Gemini who loves a Leo, contemplate the following:

✧ Are you truthful, in a loving way, with your lion?

✧ Do you accept responsibility for your life?

✧ Are you two able to laugh together?

✧ What do you love about this union?

Leo–Libra

RULED BY THE SUN AND VENUS

This match is smiled upon by the stars. Dazzling Leo is ruled by the Sun, and Libra is governed by Venus, which means these signs combined bring a unique fusion of heart, strength, beauty, and love. They are totally compatible.

They will spend excessively, however, unless one or both has the Moon, Mercury, Mars, or rising sign in Virgo or Capricorn to curb such extravagance. A Libra appreciates art and expensive cars or clothes and has a yearning for the finer things in life, and a Leo loves bling, so the more money they have to spend on paintings and Persian rugs with which to fill their rather large house(s), the more harmonious this match will be. I'm not saying they are shallow, though; both will jump to defend someone in need or rise to a worthy cause, but they do like nice things. If they both can indulge each other regularly, it will make the notes from the harp in their living room (the one standing next to the grand piano) sound even lovelier.

The main drawback is that all planets orbit the sun; the fact that Venus gets closer to it than most others (aside from Mercury) is relevant because a Libra and a Leo will have to become close enough to get together. But nobody can fly too close to the sun without getting burned. A Libra, ruled by Venus, isn't afraid, intimidated, or concerned about being outshone. They have their own subtle blend of charm and dazzle that they can weaponize, should they so wish. A Leo doesn't appreciate being eclipsed by anyone, so the fact that a Libra is usually happy to take a back seat and shine in their own right suits the lion just fine; it's rarely competitive.

A Leo fully expects a Libra, like Venus, to revolve around them, and everything else should be secondary. A Libra doesn't need as much public recognition as a Leo but is used to being fawned over by a lover, so there may just be a little trouble in paradise if this becomes unbalanced. And lions do get jealous. If they feel they can't trust their lover, they will leave; if they can't leave, all hell breaks loose, regularly.

ATTRACTION

A Libra (ruled by the goddess of art, love, and beauty) initially respects anything, or anyone, that looks good. We all know beauty is only skin deep, but to these beings, it's very important, and they are unlikely to look twice until someone wows them. A Leo almost always glitters enough to light up the darkest room. When they see that a Libra has recognized their special blend of gorgeous, the initial attraction is set.

REACHING NIRVANA

A Leo is impressed by the refined manners and polished beauty of a Libra (even if a Libra isn't physically lovely, they have attractive energy), and unless they have other astro challenges, a Libra is never uncouth or vulgar, shying away from loud outbursts or public displays and quick to distance themselves from people who will vex their gentle souls. For this reason, a Leo must be reserved in public and make a point of working through any personal issues privately and without temper tantrums.

A Libra needs to charm and tame their lion with love and patience, never neglecting them physically or emotionally.

Both could do with a joint interest, like hiking, yoga, working out, or meditation, to keep the flames alive.

If you are a Leo who loves a Libra, contemplate the following:

✧ What attracted you to your Libra?

✧ If you could change one thing about them, what would that be?

✧ What do you think they would want to change about you?

✧ Are you able to love them passionately and compassionately?

✧ What does unconditional love mean to you?

If you are a Libra who loves a Leo, contemplate the following:

✧ What attracted you to your Leo? Are any of your reasons purely superficial?

✧ Do you withdraw from your lion or neglect them? If so, why? Can you work through this calmly?

✧ Do you have shared interests and hobbies?

✧ Do you feel peaceful in this union? If yes, fab! If no, what can you do to address this?

Leo–Aquarius

RULED BY THE SUN AND SATURN/URANUS

There's never a dull moment when these colossal stars collide, as opposite signs on the zodiac wheel often do. Opposite signs are learning similar lessons in life and often have traits that would benefit the other.

This union is best if the Leo has a planet in Aquarius and vice versa because then they will tolerate each other a little more, or at least have a vague idea of where the other is coming from, which is a miracle with any Aquarius. They don't set out to shock, but they can and they do, and there is no sign that completely personifies the word *random* like they do. A Leo must shake a mane and tail to keep up, and although this is tolerable for friendships, it can become disconcerting to the point that their roars of outrage will be heard in the neighboring zip code.

To paint a picture: a Leo is giving one of their long lectures on whatever has happened to them that day, or on why the Aquarius ought to behave more like them, or why they were in the right, expecting that the Aquarius will agree, pacify, sympathize, or congratulate the lion on what they said. But the Aquarius has already got the gist, put on their coat, laced up their roller skates, and hit the pavement before the Leo has even gotten to the ending. In short, the Leo rarely will get their ego plumped or pumped by an Aquarius, so it's better that they don't even try.

An Aquarius could learn warmth of heart and how to command respect and playful affection from their Leo, whereas this lion also could do with even a small amount of the wave maker's humility, perceptiveness, humanity, and irreverence toward fame and status. If each has at least a rising sign, or planet, in the other's sign, then maybe they will have a smidge of insight into the otherwise baffling behavior they may encounter. But the tendency to gravitate toward our own star signs (which also represent our ego) is usually strong.

When either sign is unevolved, it's often ugly. The Leo is a borderline narcissist, jealously competitive and loose with their lips and other people's privacy. As for the Aquarius, if they have an afflicted Mercury in their full charts, or Gemini taking over, they gladly will trash people with the ungracious lion. All this toxicity is intolerable as far as evolved Aquarians are concerned; they loathe gossip or anything salacious, seeing right through to the spite-filled motivations of the messenger. Although they view the lions (or folks with Leo Moon/Venus/rising, etc.) afflicted with these mindplosions with compassion, they end up giving them a wide berth. There is no chance of any intimacy, let alone a marriage.

Noble lions are well matched with the right side of Aquarius because they are equally as intolerant of low-vibe humans. They try to see the best in humanity and bravely defend the underdogs. They also will stand by the wave maker's side to fiercely fight all wrongs and misjustices, as one.

COMPASSIONATE LOVE
Aquarius sees past most humans' bad behavior, or at least they review it logically and compassionately to ascertain why, which the Leo finds strange, as they are prone to react first and think later.

Most lions stick to their word, especially those who gravitate more toward a masculine energy. They are unforgiving of bad behavior and strong in their judgments. If someone is out in the cold, there would have been a jolly good reason (so they say), and that's where they stay until they "learn their lesson," which may be never if it's an Aquarius. In this battle of wills, it's unlikely that either will win because both would rather starve than give in, and "sorry" doesn't come easily to a Leo. On the flip side, if an Aquarius is wrong, they confess, or if they feel bad for the lion they may offer an olive branch. But if it's always them smoothing feathers and fur, they'll soon get fed up and move on.

Feminine lions are more forgiving, if not as naturally as wave makers (unless they have afflicted Scorpio planets), who can forgive crimes or betrayals most others would consider unthinkable. They value freedom above all else, and to be locked into a negative state of anger doesn't make any sense to them. A Leo finds this amusing but also admirable, and they can learn a great deal here. This ability to detach from emotion and rationalize human behavior (unless they have Cancer rising or Moon signs) means the Aquarius stands steady in the face of the Leo outburst, never taking it too personally. They can empathize with the pain of their hurt lion but rarely fail to let them know when they are wrong or tell them it is their ego that is wounded, not their mortality. A Leo adores, and detests, this accountability in equal measure.

REACHING NIRVANA

Noble lions are thoughtful, wise, strong, and proud, with good reason, and they are captivated by the wave maker's unique quirks, innate kindness, and sense of humanity. An Aquarius falls in love with their lion heart. It's unlikely that they have ever encountered such devotion, loyalty, fun, or love from another, and this encourages them to come down from their space station to closely observe this creature and try to understand them. It's so sweet.

An Aquarius requires trust before intimacy, and when a Leo earns this, it will prevent any Aquarian coldness from kicking in. An Aquarius must be present with their love and become more affectionate, taking time to stroke their lion between them both saving the world.

If you are a Leo who loves an Aquarius, contemplate the following:

✧ Do you drone on about yourself? If so, are you aware that you do?

✧ Do you chase recognition? If so, why? Isn't doing a good deed enough? Why do you need praise?

✧ What do you love about your wave maker?

If you are an Aquarius who loves a Leo, contemplate the following:

✧ Are you patient with your lover?

✧ What do you love about your lion?

✧ What are your major flaws in love unions?

Sagittarius–Gemini
RULED BY JUPITER AND MERCURY

The archer and the twin can't help but gravitate toward each other with an instant attraction that transcends time and place. They almost feel compelled to form an association; the only person who exists for each is the other. It's sweet but problematic if either is already spoken for. If both are evolved, then there is no problem; they both have integrity and will work to clean up their affairs before they engage in anything less than wholesome and will be kind and honest to all parties. Most people adhere to worldly and societal policies, but the laws that have much longer-lasting consequences are spiritual. It is against spiritual law to engage in any sexual activity that may hurt the self or others. It may seem that some folks (mostly Gemini or Sagittarius) get away with infidelity and other bad behavior, but even they do not. This is only one life of many, and we each carry with us all the good, and the bad, deeds of our past into the present, and our present into future incarnations, which is why it's so vital that the Sagittarius and Gemini (and everyone else) don't allow unbridled, selfish desires to steer them toward bad decisions.

The archer's main life lessons lie within the realms of truth and spirituality, so anything less than honest won't result in joy in the long term. After all, an archer is ruled by Jupiter, the judge, and a Gemini is ruled by Mercury, the messenger, or the trickster, depending on the mood. A Gemini is also learning about the effects of truth and the inner workings of the mind. Although they seemingly do not share in the boomerang effects of karma quite as swiftly as an archer, its all-seeing eye will eventually spot them, and it's far better for them to clean up their life, too.

ADVENTURE

These two signs are opposite each other on the zodiac wheel, which means that one often possesses traits and qualities the other doesn't but probably ought to. They also are studying the same lessons at the college of life, just from different perspectives.

The archer is free-spirited and independent, often wise, and uncannily prophetic, but they are powerless in the face of a Gemini—or the two faces of a Gemini, I should say. They both ignite excitement in the other and may run off into the sunset holding hands before either has had time to consider the consequences, or anyone or anything else.

This is such a lovely and lively relationship when it's working well. They encourage each other to explore greater opportunities, gain knowledge, become better people, and maybe even get involved in worthy causes. When they combine, life becomes a more thrilling experience.

REACHING NIRVANA

When they decide to bring out the best versions of themselves with loving-kindness, compassion, tolerance, and forgiveness, all will be well. That means the archer must avoid self-righteous or judgmental mannerisms, and the Gemini needs to show patience and kindness. Archers may go over the top or to extremes, and for this reason, it's wise for them to adopt healthy habits and a moderation for any habits that don't serve them particularly well. A Gemini must train their mind to become less discursive and disruptive; the more focused the twin is on the law of gratitude in general, the more they will amplify their reasons to be grateful.

Faith is an important factor here, and if they can find a joint version of higher truth, even better. Otherwise, a search to find one may be a binding and more fulfilling quest for them both.

If you are a Sagittarius who loves a Gemini, contemplate the following:

✧ Are you ever self-righteous?

✧ Do you go to extremes?

✧ What do you love about your Gemini?

✧ Are you able to laugh together?

If you are a Gemini who loves a Sagittarius, contemplate the following:

✧ Do you push your archer into doing what you want to do?

✧ What do you love about your archer? Past and present.

✧ Are you patient with your lover?

✧ If they have bad habits, do you direct them toward getting help?

Sagittarius–Libra
RULED BY JUPITER AND VENUS

The archer and the virgin—they may not seem to have a lot in common, but this is a pretty good match when you look behind the facade.

An archer is ruled by Jupiter, known as the judge (and also the jury at times), and a Libra (the scales) is ruled by Venus, who is depicted blindfolded, holding the scales of justice. Her eyes are covered so she isn't influenced or prejudiced by what she may see and, therefore, can deliver a fair assessment of the facts. A Libra generally is reasonable and rational in all matters, including affairs of the heart, which appeals to the archer, especially those who may have been faced with overly emotional lovers in the past. If a Libra has strong water signs featuring in their full charts, this may be lessened somewhat, as it would with a fiery Moon, which may lead to passion overruling logic.

Evolved, a Libra abhors any form of discrimination or unfairness, and when this is the case, an archer can learn how to become a better version of themselves. Likewise, when an archer is evolved, they have the ability and the razor-sharp tongue necessary to shoot down any bias and can debate in ways that open hearts and minds to the reality of our human equality. When the two team up, they can become the most powerful combination on Earth to carry out peaceful protests and foment progress. Of course, the unevolved versions are the opposite of all that—yet even they have the chance to become enlightened. Falling in love opens their minds for long enough to eventually see sense and reason.

This combination can result in two idealistic, adorable humans who light up every room they enter and have Lady Luck shining on them wherever they go. They are able to create their own Utopia with a blend of freedom, devotion, and commitment that will hold them together. They also have an incredible ability to land on their feet.

EXTRAVAGANCE

This combo of fire and air also may result in ignorant, bigoted, judgmental, and intolerant beings who are like the human equivalent of goblins—those mischievous spirits made of fire and air sent to cause arguments and disruption simply because it's fun to do so.

Archers may be the wandering type. If they are honest, they will not stray, or will at least try to form a union that will fit with their character and still fulfill the needs of their Libra. The Libra usually bowls them over to the point that they truly believe they can hang up their hiking boots. But that is unlikely to last for a lifetime, unless they partake in some serious self-improvement. A Libra is more tolerant than most, but they do expect fealty, and archers have a rough ride ahead if they want to avoid the blindfold coming off, revealing the devastating glare of a disappointed Libra.

Both can be overindulgent, whether that looks like spending too much on expensive gifts or on their lives in general. They charter helicopters and drive the flashiest of polluting vehicles, all in the name of pleasure. They can either help each other become more moderate or exaggerate the desire for fast thrills; it all depends on the maturity of their souls.

REACHING NIRVANA

An archer is clever, and a Libra is cool-headed and logical enough to handle, support, *and* keep them interested, which is a miracle.

The Libra fans the flames of passion while encouraging their archer toward greatness, and vice versa.

Archers are proud of their scales, especially their fairness, gentle demeanor, and achievements. Rarely do archers feel jealous or resentful (unless they have a Scorpio/Taurus/Aries Moon, Mars, or rising sign), and this results in a stable, balanced, and loving relationship.

Ignorance cannot play a part for either of them, so both need to quench their thirst for knowledge by searching out higher wisdom, attempting to journey with their soul and explore what love without expectations looks like.

If you are a Sagittarius who loves a Libra, contemplate the following:

✧ Does your lover help you be more objective?

✧ Are you aware of your lover's needs?

✧ Do you both take each other into consideration when making decisions?

If you are a Libra who loves a Sagittarius, contemplate the following:

✧ Does your lover excite you?

✧ Are you in love with your archer? If so, why?

✧ Is this union balanced? If not, how can you both address this?

Sagittarius–Aquarius
RULED BY JUPITER AND SATURN/URANUS

This is a multidimensional meeting of higher minds, and there is rarely any doubt that the archer and wave maker are completely enthralled with each other. The archer ignites the wave maker's mental faculties with flames of excitement and passion, and the Aquarius makes those flames grow higher with all the brain power they can muster. The passion can be steamy, but it's much more likely that this relationship will begin as a platonic friendship, with both constantly testing the intelligence, beliefs, and credibility of the other. This cerebral tennis match may prove too much for any other signs, but not these two. They go on and on and on. For them, this is foreplay at its very best. The archer teaches the wave maker tolerance, and the archer gets to learn all about the healing effect of compassion from the Aquarius.

A Sagittarius has many different faces; one is ignorant or uneducated, and another is purely academic. And then we have the well-rounded archer, who understands that the more they learn, the more they realize how little they actually know. When that realization sets in, they become truly receptive and able to benefit from an association with this strange but marvelous being.

The unevolved Aquarian is equally as unpleasant as an ignorant archer. They are fixed, opinionated without facts, extreme, and elitist, so you can see why either evolved or unevolved they would attract each other, for better or for worse.

INTELLECTUAL PROWESS

Archers cannot come to terms with the fact that there could be another person, outside their own sign, with as much sass, random yet factual knowledge, and strength of spirit necessary to fly freely in the face of normality.

Both Sagittarians and Aquarians are painfully honest (unless there are Mercury aspects in their full charts), which can be perceived as hurtful by other signs. This gives them a commonality and a rare appreciation of each other. They share an optimistic outlook and are ready to face the future without fear. That lack of fear can lead to taking some hair-raising risks, which often pay off, much to the surprise of more risk-adverse folk.

They inspire and encourage each other in equal measure. Any problems that may arise are mainly ego related (which is the case for 99.9 percent of relationship issues) as both fight for dominance, freedom, or the award for "being right." They delight in the art of debate; while everyone else has fallen asleep or lost the thread, these two will carry on gleefully, drawing on information from far-flung planets. This is usually how they bind, and if one lacks the intellectual prowess to keep up, it's unlikely that the union will last. Forever is far too long to spend with a lover who lacks intelligence.

REACHING NIRVANA

With energy levels that match each other, this partnership can be incredibly stimulating. For this union to be transcendent and develop into enduring love, their intellect must be relatively equal to ensure that their mutual respect endures. The friendship is likely to last, but as far as physical stimulation goes, more work may be needed to counteract boredom or wanderlust, which both parties will need to curb.

Studying spirituality and the works of sages and prophets is a way for the two to continue bringing something interesting to the table. They also need freedom and trust as well as the ability to renegotiate the terms and conditions of their partnership, should things become imbalanced.

If you are a Sagittarius who loves an Aquarius, contemplate the following:

✧ Do you always believe you are right?

✧ What do you love about your wave maker?

✧ Do you allow your partner the same amount of independence you expect for yourself?

If you are an Aquarius who loves a Sagittarius, contemplate the following:

✧ Are you fixed in your own beliefs? If so, does that stifle your growth?

✧ What do you appreciate about your archer?

✧ Does your lover inspire you?

Water and Earth Signs Combined
Cancer–Taurus
RULED BY THE MOON AND VENUS/GAIA

You may wonder what a tough-skinned old bull and a soft-shelled crab have in common, but it's rather a lot. They are similar in nature and life goals and have many complementary characteristics. They are drawn together in ways that a Cancer will happily explain as fate, karma, destiny, or bad luck, depending on their lunar-ruled mood. A bull will shrug and smile, saying that the Cancer is being "soppy" or silly, but really, they know it, too.

Intuitively, a Cancer knows that a Taurus will provide for them forever, if they give their bull what they need: nice things, amazing sex, delicious food, comfort, and consistency. The Taurus is usually the better chef; they are usually reticent to part with their hard-earned cash (unless they have Leo Moon/rising or some sort of extravagant placement), but for food, well, that's different. It's fuel, it's practical, and it makes sense to fill one's tank with the finest nourishment—and they are all about nourishment: organic, fresh, locally sourced, and plentiful. Whereas bulls may have been too busy chasing their tails to figure out that the food they consume impacts their energy, mood, and strength, a Cancer will have worked that one out long ago and will only disclose the amount they spent (from the joint account) on clothes after the bull has a full belly. It sounds old-fashioned, but believe me, it's astro factual.

VALUES

These signs have similar values, like security, family, and the wish to settle into something that resembles "respectable" normality. In short, they are traditional at heart.

The Cancer is concerned, intuitive, and kind and veers toward the more divine/creative feminine energy. The same goes for the Taurus; they are ruled by Venus, after all, or they may be more aligned with co-ruler Gaia/Mother Earth. If the latter, it's vital that they either live in the countryside away from pollution and noisy bustle, or they spend daily time outside, walking in nature, hugging trees, and sniffing flowers.

If they find themselves confined to a city, they may become out of touch with their gracious natures and run the risk of becoming hard-nosed bulls with more than a sprinkle of aggression and anger. The Cancer will look the other way in this case because they know all about emotional explosions. But as long as the bull is not physically violent, and if the Cancer is getting what they want (usually security) from this union, they simply will turn the other cheek.

REACHING NIRVANA

The unfathomable love between these two transcends the ordinary. It's unexplainable, but it soothes both of these souls who may have previously lacked nourishment or stability. They are sympathetic to each other in ways that neither can fully explain, and they feel a karmic draw to create a stable life together.

Now, one may wrongly assume that the bull is in charge, but the Cancer always gets what they want. They can be quietly controlling. For this reason, the Cancer must care for the bull and express their needs, too, so all stays balanced.

Bulls benefit from energy-releasing exercises such as qigong or yoga, and the Cancer ought to focus on taming their mind with daily meditation and prayer.

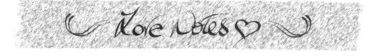

If you are a Cancer who loves a Taurus, contemplate the following:

✧ Do you express your needs in this relationship? Best results are achieved with patience, consistency, kindness, and love.

✧ What do you love about your bull?

✧ Do you see how food impacts your bull's energy?

✧ Do you meditate? If yes, fab. If not, try it for ten days and note any differences.

✧ Are you controlling? If yes, why? If not, really? Never ever?

If you are a Taurus who loves a Cancer, contemplate the following:

✧ What do you love about your Cancer?

✧ Do you make moves to show your crab that you care?

✧ Do you spend time in nature? If not, you must make the time.

✧ Do you exercise? Have you tried gentle movements? Try qigong or yoga for a week, and note any differences in your energy and flexibility.

Cancer–Virgo

RULED BY THE MOON AND MERCURY/CHIRON

The lunar baby and the virgin sounds idyllic, and it certainly can be. Evolved virgins are pure of spirit, protect love fearlessly, and care deeply about their loved ones, which suits the sensitive lunar child, who is prone to feeling uncared for, misunderstood, and emotionally neglected by most prior lovers. Both signs are special, and just as talent recognizes other talent, special knows its own reflection. When an open-hearted crab chances upon the delectable virgin, they forge a fortress to defend against the harsher aspects of life and keep them safe from negative influences.

Crabs are the most nurturing of signs, but subtly, without smothering their Virgo, by doing everything from clearing and cleaning the energy in the home, to exposing and weeding out toxic influences in their lives. They know how to take care of a Virgo, and without their Virgo even knowing how much they do behind the scenes. The truth is that the Virgo rarely misses a trick; they just don't always talk about it. Like siblings with their own language, a Cancer enables a Virgo to dial into their "energy speak" and read vibes rather than needing words. It's the most intimate form of communication.

EXPECTATIONS

Virgins have extremely high expectations (like their fellow Venus-ruled sign, Libra), and a Cancer will rise to meet them if they also feel that flash of instant recognition, as if they have known this person before, in a not-too-distant past life—a soul mate, perhaps.

Both signs are security conscious, so if money is no problem, that certainly helps. It's important that they work on give and take and agree early on about how practical life matters will be addressed so that there is no room for arguments or misunderstandings.

When a Virgo is in their flow, they are cool, chill, laid back, and confident. Now, we all know virgins who are anxiety and mania personified, but truly, that's not what they were star-sent to Earth to become. That is a very low vibration, and if any virgin reading this forgets how bright their shimmer is, they should know that it's vital to their love lives and essential for their souls that they rise up and step into their sexy rock-star guise.

Virgins who suffer from the chatter of insecurity or worry still will attract a Cancer, but usually it's the mothering, insecure version of the crab, which isn't sexy, nor sustainable. The *need to be needed* is suffocating, and all actions are simply reactions to boost their own self-esteem. The problem with those who suffer with self-esteem issues is that they are so disconnected from their source energy, they subconsciously try to steal it from others. Unevolved virgins are fearful control freaks with sharp, spiteful tongues, and if they attract the low-vibe crab, they'll snipe and side-swipe in tandem. They make a "happy" match, but only in their mutual misery.

Evolved, the Cancer is a completely different story. A Cancer is as cool as a Virgo, quietly intuitive, rock-solid in their confidence, kind, and creative with the ability to laugh at themselves, life, and the universe. It's the ultimate form of attraction for a Virgo because they may be prone to taking life a tad too seriously.

REACHING NIRVANA

It's as if the moon goddess herself, Mercury, the messenger of gods, and Cupid have conspired to bedazzle this pair into opening their hearts to love. It's really romantic, and that is crystal clear from early on. If both continue to put in the effort, that romance will stay alive and soon be accompanied by enduring love.

Both must work on their own confidence levels so they never attempt to dim the light of the other, and dialing into a higher faith is important for them. It doesn't matter if they share the same faith, but they must find their own way and realize that the very nature of impermanence, which will give them soul confidence, also prevents either of them from ever taking each other, or a single moment of happiness, for granted.

If you are a Cancer who loves a Virgo, contemplate the following:

✧ Do you nurture your love and your lover? How?

✧ How is your self-esteem? What do you do to keep it high?

✧ Do you practice spirituality?

❖ What is your definition of karma?

❖ Is your virgin your soul mate?

If you are a Virgo who loves a Cancer, contemplate the following:

❖ Are you evolved? Or working toward it?

❖ Do you ever become controlling? If so, why? What are you afraid of?

❖ Do you and your lover laugh together? Make room for humor.

❖ Are you prone to criticize in your idealistic search for perfection? If so, stop and kick the habit!

Cancer–Capricorn
RULED BY THE MOON AND SATURN

The graceful goat and the lunar baby are starred to form a union that brings them in from the metaphorical cold to bask in the warm luminosity of the moon. When they are together and have both decided to commit, their love brightens up the darkness of the night sky.

As opposite signs on the zodiac wheel, they each may bring to the other what may be required for them to fulfill their soul's obligation or mission.

Saturn-ruled goats are in the dark for many reasons, but mainly because their ruling planet is cold, demanding, and austere—until they encounter their Moon-ruled deity, and then everything begins to take on a new patina of possibility, heralding change and progress.

The Cancer also feels alone in the dark, for many reasons. They fear coming out into the bright sunshine just in case they are *seen* or get hurt. They wear a mask of toughness that conceals their kindness and generosity of spirit, and hide underneath their shells, only venturing out at night to forage. They don't miss the daylight; for them, night is the time when the sun steps aside and allows the moon to shine. They bring a different sort of light to their Capricorn's life; it's less intimidating than the blinding light of a Leo yet still all-encompassing, which nourishes their goat and invigorates their energy. They happily reciprocate by ramping up the unconditional love and kindness and doing all they can to protect their crab and their sensitivity to vibes, people, and life.

AMBITIONS

If a Cancer has Aquarius or Sagittarius featuring prominently in their full natal charts, this makes their desire for adventure, fun, and freedom supersede everything else. Without a sprinkling of air and fire, they are too focused on material and/or emotional security, which means they often have needs above and beyond the basic requirements for a humble life. Our mindset at the time of our death predetermines our next incarnation. Often that desire is in them before birth, so they land in a family who are already wealthy, or at the least have fame or status.

If a Capricorn has a Moon or rising sign in Capricorn, it works better for the union in the long term because they have the ability to feel more than one who doesn't. It also calms the ambition and ruthless nature that often plague the poor goats, causing them much suffering and bad karmic results. The same goes for the Cancer. When they have a Moon, or rising sign, or any other planet in Capricorn, it gives them an attractive level of reserve and discernment so they can rise above lower ego's trap of taking things too personally and overreacting.

If a Cancer has a Leo Moon or Venus, they are more likely to become attached to a goat who is already financially secure or on the path to greatness. Even if the Cancer is successful in their own right, they will have an underlying fear of past-life poverty, be it emotional or material, driving them to make the right choice in a partner—one who won't leave them physically or bankrupt them in any way. A Capricorn is keen to make a mark in the world, and if their Cancer can help them do that, they will overlook any of the warning flags and pledge their allegiance.

A Cancer desires a comfortable life, and goats are as good at providing as their fellow earth sign Taurus, so on the surface, this makes for a fortuitous union. But we must question where love is in all of this because they both need it. Goats must beware that their sure-footed steps are not trampling all over their Cancer in their desire for gain, and the Cancer must communicate in a nonemotional but heartfelt way before they clam up, overreact, and find solace elsewhere.

Goats can be hard and a Cancer soft, so the answer lies somewhere in between. They must be careful not to destroy each other, for karma is swift.

REACHING NIRVANA
For it to work in the long term, this must be a balanced and mutually rewarding union.

Letting go of attachments is the only approach. Opening their hearts and communicating with love and compassion will help them transcend the barrenness of a life based on superficiality. Recognizing the beauty in each other and aligning their souls will help, as will a strong sense of spiritual faith, which can only really arrive after research and contemplation.

If you are a Cancer who loves a Capricorn, contemplate the following:

✦ What attracted you to your lover? What still attracts you?

✦ Is your partner kind? If yes, great. If not, can they change?

✦ Do you laugh with your lover? This is important.

✦ Do you feel emotionally secure in this union? If so, make notes. If not, why not?

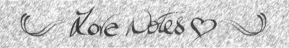

If you are a Capricorn who loves a Cancer, contemplate the following:

✦ What attracted you to your lover? Was it them? Or what they may provide?

✧ What do you love about your crab?

✧ Do you know how to relax together? If so, how? If not, why?

Scorpio–Taurus
RULED BY MARS/PLUTO AND VENUS/GAIA

Scorpio and Taurus are opposite and fixed signs that result in a palpable energetic attraction. This combination gives a partnership an incredible power surge, supercharging the potential to become great together, and a unique opportunity for real spiritual growth. If the latter is of no interest, it could get a little messy as they struggle to assert dominance, which is a shame because they each have so much to learn and gain from the other. To use their combined force to gain worldly power and status—which is relatively easy for them as a duo—is indeed an opportunity missed.

The lessons imparted are not always comfortable because they involve facing their shadows. Neither particularly likes to do this, although bulls are far more honest and open about their shortcomings. When push comes to shove, they face a challenge head-on.

A Scorpio is not very good at saying "sorry" (they share that trait with fellow fixed sign Leo). They feel that flaws are weakness, and that terrifies them. To them, weakness could be fatal, so unless they are an evolved scorpion, they will scheme or fight to the death rather than face their shadows and faults. The problem is that they see far beyond the face another presents—they know what motivates a person and can read a room in seconds. However, if they have no faith to protect them, if they are tired or fail to clean their own energy and heal themselves, then their penetrating eyes are blind to the light and all they see in others is darkness.

When they encounter the straightforward honesty of a Taurus, it inspires them to consider becoming more like them, which is where the growth area lies. A Taurus knows exactly how to heal; they remove themselves from the bombardment of life and plod along in nature, unplugged and content, which is exactly what a Scorpio needs. Of course, if they have Taurus planets, they've likely already learned this and probably met their bull lover at the local farmers market.

If a Scorpio is truly strong, they are honest, confident, and magnificent with an irresistible magnetism that draws in their Taurus and makes them fall majestically in love. Nothing will break that karmic bond. They vow on a soul level to help each other overcome all sorts of challenges. This is a stronger connection than most, giving them the ability to hold hands and pull each other out of the worldly muck that would otherwise obscure them from seeing the bigger, and much brighter, picture.

DISCIPLINE

When one thinks of the relationship between a bull and a scorpion, all sorts of qualities come to mind. The only one that ought to stick is this: they both have extremely long memories, and despite their difference in size, the scorpion is probably the most dangerous.

If you wrong either, they will not forget it. The Taurus, however, will give you the opportunity to put it right, if they feel you are worth it. The scorpion will flash those smoldering eyes and say they forgive, or that it's fine, but really, you are on their list now. The only one who can talk them into letting it go is their Taurus. There is a trust in this relationship that nourishes them both, and the love that grows as a result is unlikely to falter.

When these two get together, there is no fear of the other. If the Taurus has a Moon or rising sign in Scorpio, and the Scorpio shares a planet with the bull, they stand a real chance of building a relationship based on respect, trust, and a powerful sexual attraction that lasts throughout the years—as long as both stay fit and lean. Neither Scorpio nor Taurus holds much respect for a partner who lets themselves go or switches healthy living for total indulgence. Both pride themselves on their discipline, and when they are working with the right side of their sign, they possess copious amounts of it.

If, however, they are not, they are driven and controlled by their desires, which is a sure bet for ruin. The Taurus may be greedy and the Scorpio selfish, and they are both prone to suffering at the hands of ugly jealousy. Bulls assume the green eye of simmering envy and may become resentful of others or possessive of their lover. The Scorpio masks it at all costs and decides instead to quietly control, belittle, or manipulate.

On a lighter note, when these two are evolved, they love without reservation, have brilliant humor, and value honor, so all that poison is left on the shelf. It's still there, but it's safely locked away.

REACHING NIRVANA

Both partners are passionate, and when they feel they have found their soul mate, they devote their lives to each other—the mutual devotion is unquestionable.

Bulls are almost always beautiful in some way, and also sensual, and the Scorpio is sexy and alluring. Both are tenacious. Although many wrongly state that bulls are aggressive and prone to bully, this is not their natural character at all. There is a huge difference between aggression and assertion; the former is when one person denies by force the actions, speech, or rights of another, and a Taurus can't be bothered with that. The evolved ones are gracious beings who have their own plans and ways of doing things; all their Scorpio needs to do is to stroke them in the right place, and they are sold for life. They are assertive and strong, and this is what attracts their Scorpio like a magnet.

To overcome their troublesome flaws that may be magnified in this union, it's vital to meditate and find a teacher who can show them how to do this properly. In adopting disciplined spiritual practice and studying the law of cause and effect, they will purify their karma for the present and for their future lives together.

Love Notes

If you are a Scorpio who loves a Taurus, contemplate the following:

✧ What attracted you to your lover?

✧ Do you suffer from jealousy? If yes, get some help because this poisons your goodness.

✧ Do you laugh at yourself? It's helpful not to take yourself too seriously!

✧ If you had a magic wand, what would you wish for?

If you are a Taurus who loves a Scorpio, contemplate the following:

✧ Does your lover bring out the best version of you?

✧ What do you value most in this union?

✧ Do you spend time in nature? Together?

✧ Are your habits healthy?

✧ Do you meditate?

Scorpio–Virgo
RULED BY MARS/PLUTO AND MERCURY/CHIRON

The relationship between the virgin and the scorpion is compli-cated (no surprise there!), and whether it's as friends, family, or lov-ers, their success and harmony wholly depends on the interplay of other signs in their full charts.

These two are sympathetic toward each other, protective even, and undeniably drawn to each other. It may seem that they are too different to make any sort of intimacy work, but that isn't the case. Virgins, in their flow, have an innocence and youthfulness that lasts for life. They are controlling, perhaps, but open and truthful in their conduct—unless, of course, they have a Scorpio planet that is not well placed close to their Sun sign, in which case they may hide a sting behind their smile.

A Virgo would probably need to have an inner planet, like the

Moon or Venus, or a rising sign in Scorpio to be able to stay connected and tolerant of the suspicious and brooding scorpion. No matter how light and breezy the latter may seem, still waters run deep in this case. That is, unless the Scorpio has Sagittarius factoring strongly in their natal chart, or other fire and air sign placements overriding those traits; they will be much lighter humans, likely to be momentarily outraged by the above slander, no doubt. But dwelling in the past for too long, like the typical grudge-bearing water sign, is not how they choose to live. They laugh at the suggestions, shake off the accusations, and carry on.

LIGHTNESS

The Virgo helps the Scorpio lighten up, and because they are such a virtuous human, this enables the Scorpio to open their heart and trust in the power of love, which is nearly impossible with other signs.

They may succumb to their shadow side, but they are not here on Earth to live a superficial life; they are here to get under the skin of life itself. They have the capacity to open people's hearts and minds, and that is where the Virgo can become interested, because they are all about the analytical workings of the human psyche. The Virgo is super analytical, and the Scorpio has a secret truth serum that makes them the best detectives on Earth. Together, they delight in analyzing strangers, colleagues, and friends alike.

REACHING NIRVANA

If the Virgo and Scorpio have Sagittarius or Aquarius in their charts, this relationship thrives. They laugh and poke fun at each other, playfully, which usually avoids the power struggles and heads straight to adoration, fun, and adventure, with the right twist of intensity and passion.

The main point here is this: how this union pans out very much depends on the charts of both and how they interconnect. If both are evolved, or at least trying to overcome their faults, their mutual respect is a firm foundation upon which to build a life brimming with adoration, intensity, and adventure.

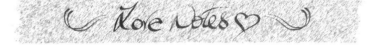

If you are a Scorpio who loves a Virgo, contemplate the following:

✧ Do you believe your lover to be honest? Does that help you open up?

✧ Are you able to laugh together?

✧ Do you have trust issues?

✧ Have you ever betrayed anyone? Has your partner? Have you forgiven yourself, or them? That's an important factor in the success of this union.

If you are a Virgo who loves a Scorpio, contemplate the following:

✧ Is this relationship intense? If yes, how does that manifest?

✧ Do you overanalyze? If yes, is this helpful? If not, can you retrain your brain?

✧ What do you love about your Scorpio? Do you ever criticize them? Or yourself? If yes, stop.

✧ Are you controlling? If so, why?

Scorpio–Capricorn
RULED BY MARS/PLUTO AND SATURN

There is something hauntingly beautiful about this association that's difficult to put into words, but I'll try. Most Scorpio children, born of Pluto, have experienced intense lives due to the nature of their ruling planet and star sign. They've had situations, very early on, that awakened them to the impermanence of life, birth, and death. Transformation is embedded in the nature of their souls, and even when surrounded by family or friends, they may feel lonely or out of place.

Capricorns are born with old souls, making them feel the weight of responsibility on their shoulders early on, and they spend the rest of their lives shrugging it all off. For that reason, they also feel lonely and a little out of place. If only they could be successful, or married and have children, or more money, they tell themselves. The goat's cycle goes on and on until they realize that the situations they are faced with are the maturation of past-life karma, for both good and not so good, and opportunities to expand their consciousness. So they must accept responsibility and learn forgiveness, which is exactly what a Scorpio must learn, too.

EMOTIONS

For both of these signs, early life experiences may mean that they bottle up their emotions, or mistrust them, so they hide them.

When a Scorpio meets a cool-headed goat who seems unflappable (unless they have neighboring signs Aquarius or Sagittarius running freely in their charts, or maybe drama-addict Leo as a rising sign, or Aries running the show), hard to read, and in control of their emotions, this thrills them because they are obsessed with what lies beneath the surface. They're like a moth to a flame when a mystery beckons, and nothing is more attractive to them than winning over a proverbial closed book. The secret, though, is that goats never allow anyone to seduce them unless they want them to, so the hypnotic and mesmerizing game for the Scorpio begins, which amuses the Capricorn no end. There are goats who lack that nous, but they are few and far between; they see the Scorpio coming before they have boarded the bus or walked through the door. As I mentioned, it's a karmic thing, and even though goats typically are not prescient, when it comes to a Scorpio, it's as if they know exactly what's coming. Maybe it's déjà vu. Scorpions have little to no idea how their schemes will play out, because the Capricorn has a better poker face than they do. So it's game, set, and quite evenly matched. When one of them falls in love, that messes things up a little because the power shifts and neither of them trusts their emotions; they both realize, on a soul level, that emotions lead to too much attachment, and they fear losing themselves and their freedom. But if the love is true, then nobody can truly lose themselves.

REACHING NIRVANA

Scorpions feel safe and proud to partner up with goats. Because their life often has been so unpredictable, the consistency of the goat and their refined manners and conservative ways soothe them, like a cool drink during a heat wave, unlike the mess of attention-seeking and dramatic past lovers.

Goats are mesmerized by the charisma of a Scorpio and, as long as both make moves to keep the routine organized but stimulating, all is well.

As with all unions, a strong faith in "what goes around comes around" is wise because it gives this duo strength and a chance to be able to purify the past and create a cleaner future, together.

If you are a Scorpio who loves a Capricorn, contemplate the following:

✧ Do you appreciate your goat? If so, how and why?

✧ Do you believe in past lives?

✧ Do you feel this union can help you grow?

✧ Are you honest with your lover? If yes, great. If not, contemplate why.

✧ What does fate mean to you?

✧ Do you know how to forgive?

If you are a Capricorn who loves a Scorpio, contemplate the following:

✧ What initially drew you to your lover?

✧ What is your greatest desire in this union?

✧ What is important to you in a partner?

✧ Do you believe in soul mates? If so, is your union with your Scorpio fated?

✧ Do you believe in karma? If so, how can you create better karma and prevent negative accumulations?

Pisces–Taurus

RULED BY JUPITER/NEPTUNE AND VENUS/GAIA

This dreamy union has a greater chance of becoming reality if the Pisces has at least one planet in Taurus and the opposite for Taurus. If that is the case, they often are attracted to each other by a mutual love of art, music, film, and creativity. This combination is tantamount to alchemy when actualizing intangible ideas that many could only ever dream of. These two can make wonderful things happen when the Taurus takes the Pisces's fin in their hoof and makes a pact to turn their world, and ours, into a better, gentler, and more creative place.

If the Taurus lacks a sensitive soul, it can be a large ask for this land-loving, materialistic bull to take a relationship with an ocean lover like the fish seriously for long. One is rooted to the earth, and the other to the abyss of the intangible, so it's going to be hard to form an association that does anything other than leave the fish frustrated and confused and the bull completely out of their depth.

Equally, there are fish who have too many earth signs in their charts. They also may fail to attune to the sensitive notes of their souls, which results in a miserable existence as they try to assert their own boundaries on others, drowning in their own fear as they become control freaks—or worse, abusive. Or they attract those types of partners, so low is their opinion of self. This usually only happens if their own boundaries have been blurred or violated as a child; they then continue in the cycle.

Fish may wallow in self-pity or victim-like behavior, which infuriates bulls. They don't tolerate either, not when there are new fresh pastures to explore and hay to munch on.

CREATIVITY

This is a stellar combination for an artist and management relationship.

Fish in their flow (or those with strong Pisces planets in their charts) are the most imaginative souls on Earth. They draw inspiration from the stars and heavens, generating pure, intuitive art, made solely for the sake of its beauty and its capacity to compel humans into an awelike state. This authentic process has nothing to do with mortal money or mass-marketing; Pisces, the true version of the sign, is all about the art, and they make unbelievable sacrifices for it. Rarely do they care for luxury. As long as they can create, little else matters (unless they have an earth sign Moon or rising sign; then money will certainly matter).

Being Venus born, the Taurus is also multitalented, but they have different priorities. They require comfort and demand compensation for their efforts. For that reason, when the two signs team up, they can part oceans and move mountains. It's both lucrative and inspiring.

REACHING NIRVANA

When both signs share a sprinkling of the other's cosmic blessings, it's a harmonious union that nourishes them in ways they never may have experienced before. Bulls become gentler versions of themselves by association, and fish reach new levels of understanding, compassion, and worldly success.

This union is all about the heart and communicating openly. It is the way to foment the purest form of love, one that can weather the storms of life.

Opening to spirituality may result in them becoming more creative and is a sure way to keep them together, hoof and fin, for life.

If you are a Pisces who loves a Taurus, contemplate the following:

✧ What do you love about this relationship?

✧ What frustrates you?

✧ Do you engage in escapist behavior? Is this healthy?

✧ Are you in tune with your sensitive nature? How so?

✧ Do you love art? Are you creative?

✧ Do you recognize the healing benefits of the oceans and seas?

If you are a Taurus who loves a Pisces, contemplate the following:

✧ Do you give each other space in this union?

✧ Are you gentle with your lover?

✧ Are you gentle with yourself?

✧ Contemplate the reality of impermanence. How does that change your attitude?

Pisces–Virgo

RULED BY JUPITER/NEPTUNE AND MERCURY/CHIRON

Fish and virgins are opposite signs on the zodiac wheel, and energetically, they are opposites in every way.

Fish move through life seamlessly; they always land on their feet, even though they don't have any, living by their gut instincts. When they have learned to trust their intuition, the outcome is flawless. They know when to arrive and when to leave, when to pull back, and when to show up. Fish have impeccable timing because they are attuned to the rhythms, ebbs, and flows of the universe. When they have managed to disentangle themselves from toxic connections and kick unhealthy habits, they are no longer slaves to their addictions. (This is an issue for them and fellow water sign Scorpio.) Such addictions cloud the flow of universal wisdom that's on tap for any fish not swimming away from themselves, and life itself, in a haze of smoke or other mind-altering consumables.

This is where the Virgo steps in, either in the fish's charts or as a lover, because a virgin in flow doesn't indulge in anything that would result in losing control. They are not interested and cannot fathom why anyone else would be. So they try to help the fish overcome the burden of addictions, and karmically, that's what this union is all about: cleaning up their lives to create something that's not only pure, but also based firmly in reality, with a magical brand of faith in the universe thrown in, too.

A fish may be unfocused and scattered, but a Virgo craves boundaries and routine to sidestep their neuroses. Fish secretly dream of boundaries or else a fellow fairy to ground them enough to stop them getting lost in space or going missing for a decade (although the former is only usually true if they have planets in Aquarius).

There *are* organized fish, but they always have several planets in Virgo, and there are artistic virgins with planets in Pisces. When this is the case, it's a more harmonious blend of qualities and flaws, which enables them to coexist peacefully and symbiotically.

One of my clients required a compromise with her lover. The fish wasn't going to stop chuffing pot, so the virgin suggested, at the very least, they grow their own to ensure it was pure and chemical free (sustainable, organic, and controlled). They built a business around it and then put it on the stock market. That's what happens when a Virgo and a Pisces *really* team up. If no compromise can be found, it's a push and pull until something gives; either considerable progress is made, or one of them leaves—usually the fish, because the Virgo may be called many names, but "quitter" isn't one.

EMPATHETIC

I have yet to come across a gifted artist who isn't sensitive, too; it's a prerequisite. How can you channel inspiration or master multimedia art without being open to the suggestive whispers of the most superlative form of creative expression in existence—the universal mind? This is both a gift and a curse, and Virgo energy has such boundaries that it knows when to keep those channels open and when to close them. A Pisces is clueless in that respect (like neighboring sign Aquarius and those with Pisces planets). They are always "on" and open to giving and receiving 24/7, which drains them and attracts the good, bad, and demonic. So the Virgo soon whips them into shape with loving-kindness, disguised by a sharp tongue, and gives them strict instructions on how to wear a cloak or veil, when to take it off, and the perils of keeping the receptors on for everyone. Virgins have vast empathy, too, but they value it as a commodity and don't give it away freely to anyone just because. They know, as the natural healers of the zodiac, just how costly that is. You may be startled to hear that virgins, as well as fish, are healers, but they truly are, and that is one gift they share. It's a hard job when you feel the joy, pain, and heartache of everyone you encounter, and it can take fish down into the murky waters of depression. So their Virgo helps them stop being sponges and encourages them to be aware of when and why they have nothing left to give. For that reason, this relationship is not only fated, but also imperative.

REACHING NIRVANA
The Virgo and Pisces partnership is best when they share a love for music, the arts, or anything creative. Oh, and service. They have a mission on Earth that need not be lonely or soul-wrenching; it can be creative and full of joy, too. Together, they may just find the paradisiacal blend.

Virgins are so kind, caring, and giving that they struggle to trust for fear of being taken advantage of. Fish are the most compassionate of souls, and for that reason, this union feels like finally, they have found each other. Together they may support all the waifs, strays, and broken birds the fish attracts, put them back together (while maintaining their boundaries), and live happily ever after.

If you are a Pisces who loves a Virgo, contemplate the following:

✧ Do you know how to heal yourself? Think about it.

✧ Do you live by or spend time near water? Try being close to the sea or ocean at least once a week, and note your mood.

✧ Do you see past your virgin's controlling ways and through to their pure heart?

✧ Do you take drugs or drink too much? Why?

If you are a Virgo who loves a Pisces, contemplate the following:

✧ Are you controlling with your lover? If so, why?

✧ Are you aware of your own healing abilities?

✧ Do you take care of your own heart?

✧ What do you love about this union?

✧ Do you take time to meditate?

Pisces–Capricorn
RULED BY JUPITER/NEPTUNE AND SATURN

A fish and a goat may be a rather good blend, as long as Neptune's baby has a little earth in their full chart (preferably Capricorn, but Taurus or Virgo works, too). Otherwise, the fish may be too *other-worldly* for the Capricorn. Although goats may toy with the idea of marrying a fairy or wizard, in reality, it's rarely worth a discussion. Goats don't stay in the dreamworld for long. They have little time for anything they can't see and simply have too much to do, sorting out the world, their friends, their family, their work, and so on.

If a Capricorn has in their charts a matching Pisces influence, or an Aries/Sagittarius/Gemini/Aquarius Moon or rising sign, to lighten the load of Saturn's expectations, then both have the potential to reach the enchanted forest of love, where divination is as normal as asking the time. This is what you get when you mix the Pisces brand of hope and possibility with Capricorn's pragmatism. It's alchemical and effective.

Goats have brilliant minds and dry wit, and fish love to laugh, but both have the tendency to take themselves, and life, too seriously. So if you add humor to the mix, it's a recipe for success and happiness.

Pisceans have as much, if not more, fairy dust up their sleeves than their neighbor Aquarius. Fish sprinkle it when nobody is looking, and they only run out if they forget who they are. It's as sad to see the formerly glittering fish worn down by life as watching a forlorn tiger resigned to its imprisonment in a small, dirty cage. Some goats have the same impact on fish as that cage, draining their life force so the fairy dust is no more and life becomes monotonous and devoid of magic, which is like a prison to the fish. They are forced to exist in a dull gray reality. Fish are the martyrs of the zodiac (along with Virgos) because any self-respecting air or fire sign would have busted out by now.

TRUST

Goats bring structure, stability, and focus to the fish, and the latter do have slightly tarnished reputations because some really are slippery, deceitful, tricky, and noncommittal—or subconsciously attract that behavior in their partners. But those fish are driven by fear and in the minority. They're not likely to interest a stand-up goat because in their flow, they are devoted to truth, hardworking, and faithful; they won't even cheat in a card game, let alone on the love of their life. They are often extremely trusting because they are trustworthy, and fish thrive on this type of certitude—stability in love is heavenly to them. Even though they kid themselves that they don't need it, they really do. So they offer their fealty and patiently work to build a life with their goat, one foot in the ocean and one on land, and commit to overcoming their fears about intimacy.

REACHING NIRVANA

If fish have forgotten how to dance freely in the moonlight or sing by the campfire on the beach, they must remember, fast, and take the goat with them. This soul memory loss also may happen if they are working solely with the earth in their own charts. In this case, they don't need a goat to restrict them; they will do it to themselves.

Goats can be cold, but so can fish, and when they try hard to soothe, sympathize, and emphasize, this overrides the potential to cause pain.

Goats must never get stuck in a routine or take love for granted, and the latter is true for fish, too. They also need to accept responsibility for the role they play in any disharmony and instead work to create a harmony that keeps them both committed, long term.

If you are a Pisces who loves a Capricorn, contemplate the following:

✦ Do you view your relationship as a sanctuary?

✧ What do you do to build trust and intimacy in your relationship?

✧ Do you laugh together?

✧ What do you do to protect your own sense of peace?

If you are a Capricorn who loves a Pisces, contemplate the following:

✧ How often do you look into your partner's eyes?

✧ Do you ever get stuck in the rut of routine?

✧ Do you say "thank you" for small gestures of kindness?

✧ How do you keep this union fresh?

Water and Air Signs Combined
Cancer–Gemini
RULED BY THE MOON AND MERCURY

A love match between a lunar baby and a twin galvanizes many cosmic blessings into one magical reality, especially if the Cancer has a Gemini planet, like the Moon, Venus, rising sign, or Mars, in their full natal chart. This results in a lightness of step and a sense of humor that will prevent them from taking love and life too seriously. The same goes for the Gemini. If blessed with a water or earth planet close to their mercurial and somewhat ungrounded natal sign and planets, they are typically more thoughtful and contemplative, which makes this pairing one of compassion and understanding.

TRIPPING THE LIGHT FANTASTIC

When a Cancer deletes the past and lets go of their need to control every moment or experience, they shine brightly enough to join their Gemini and trip the light fantastic; just a few days or even moments can make all the difference as they open themselves to the sheer fun and joy that only ever exists in the moment. When a Cancer looks back too often, it only makes their neck hurt.

A Gemini has an aversion to intensity and emotion, but this doesn't mean they are shallow. Although they can be, subconsciously they probably know that in their next incarnation they will be born under the sensitive, all-feeling sign of Cancer, so for now, they just want to have fun, gain knowledge, and create mischief along the way while teasing as many serious crabs as they can just because it tickles them to do so. Gemini are far too nimble on their mercurial feet to get pinched or caught in the net for too long.

REACHING NIRVANA

The best of the Cancer is gentle, generous, and kind by nature, and the clever twin ramps up these attractive traits by slowing down and taking the water baby's feelings into consideration—from time to time, at least.

The uglier, defensive side of the Cancer is negative, unkind, and downright mean, but the luminous purity of the lunar baby's spirit is *always* underneath that pain. When the Gemini dials in to their famed smarts and dazzling intelligence, they will recognize that the Cancer's overreactions and defensiveness are merely a result of their suffering, and it's never personal. As one of the smartest signs in the zodiac, the Gemini easily can see past these bad behaviors, shrug them off, and trigger the better side of their partner's nature. This is where the rule of three (Ro3) on page xvii comes into full effect. This is good karma for the Gemini and an opportunity for them to give back.

The Cancer also can amplify the love vibes by watching their own reactions and not smothering or being too possessive of their light-footed love—and certainly not taking every sentence their Gemini (and all other humans) forms as a personal dig.

Patience is the key, and an appreciation of each other's differences helps. Fewer attachments to perceptions of how the union ought to be will bring them both into the magic of the moment.

If you are a Cancer who loves a Gemini, contemplate the following:

✧ Is your sensitivity attached to your own ego or feelings? If so, take account and stop doing this or internalizing.

✧ Are you prone to be possessive of your Gemini?

✧ Do you laugh together?

✧ What do you love about your twin?

If you are a Gemini who loves a Cancer, contemplate the following:

✧ Do you consider how sensitive your Cancer is? How does this make you feel?

✧ Try to evoke your crab's kindness and generosity.

✧ Consider partaking in a joint creative project.

✧ Do you meditate? If yes, how does this help? If not, try!

Cancer–Libra
RULED BY THE MOON AND VENUS

The Libran scales of balance and the disconcertingly swift, mood-changing, lunar-ruled crab have their work cut out for them in this union, that is for sure. However, the Libra feels (initially) that they have more than enough sunshine and cheer for both, so they pour their heart, soul, and enthusiasm into this relationship for just long enough to coax the Cancer out of its skeptical shell and into the throes of romance. The Libra is probably the most sympathetic and understanding of all the air signs, which is why this match is easier than a Cancer + Aquarius or Gemini, in the short term, at least.

A Libra can be needy for love overall, and a Cancer needs to feel needed—that's a whole lot of need and insufficiency, which may lead to both grasping onto something or someone external, like a romance, to feel complete. This is a recipe for disaster. The Libra is depicted as a set of balanced scales for good reason; they require balance in all areas of life, yet some may wrongly assume that they are incomplete or unbalanced without a partner or other half.

COMPROMISE

When these two are in their flow, they have the potential to create a spectacular relationship that offers both security and a harmonious blend of compromise and loving-kindness.

A lovestruck Libra is full of affection and bursting with the joys of spring, which makes them most alluring to crabs. Their open-hearted attitude to love and life evokes the tenderhearted, softer side of the Cancer, and together, they will plan to build a solid marriage of souls that is balanced between the Cancer's preoccupation with themselves and their own feelings and the Libra's natural tendency to care what others think. They weigh the pros and cons of every person and interaction, which is an opportunity for learning for the crab, who is so persuasive they could make saints become momentarily cynical, paranoid, or mistrusting.

Crabs intuitively know that they can trust their Libra because no other sign is more well-meaning. For that reason, they get to hear two logical sides of a tale when previously it was only ever their own version. This enables them to give others (and themselves) the benefit of doubt. With this as a result, this union can be as close to perfect as any.

REACHING NIRVANA

If the Cancer can stop trying so hard to be understood and begin to try to understand, this changes the game for them with the Libra.

To lessen the grip of lower ego, both can empathize. When the Libra starts to see their lover for who they are and stops building fairy tales and sandcastles, they can assess what works, where compromise is called for, and how they may bring out the best in each other. That way, they achieve balance and a real, enduring love.

If you are a Cancer who loves a Libra, contemplate the following:

✧ Do you think you are prone to see the worst in people?

✧ Question how many times you were happily wrong about someone's intentions. Now take note.

✧ Does your lover help you see things from a different perspective?

If you are a Libra who loves a Cancer, contemplate the following:

✧ Is your union based on reality or your own fantasy of how a partnership ought to be?

✧ Do you help your lover lighten up?

✧ Can you make a vow to bring out the best in each other? What does that look like?

Cancer–Aquarius
RULED BY THE MOON AND SATURN/URANUS

This is not the easiest relationship for either the lunar baby or the wave maker. By cosmic design, they are so startlingly different and have contrasting goals and priorities. It does have plenty to bestow in terms of growth and learning, but a lasting marriage or love match is challenging unless both get to the stage where the love they feel for the other is unconditional.

A Cancer can become passive aggressive, withdrawing to take back control, and an Aquarius can become coolly detached to save their sanity from emotional combustion, unless these two have Capricorn or Taurus in their charts, which gives them the chemistry, impetus, and tenacity to fight for each other. Otherwise, this may just fizzle out due to so many misunderstandings. The Cancer gets the Aquarius all wrong, such is their suspicious nature. The Aquarius is intuitive, as opposed to merely calculating, and this latter trait is what the Cancer has spent eons perfecting. Wave makers live well by their gut instincts. It's rarely contrived; they just don't have the time to plot like a Cancer may.

A logical Aquarius finds an emotional Cancer to be a wet blanket. The former breezes through the moment and lives airily in the future and will never comprehend why a Cancer wishes to dwell in the past, especially if it was not a happy place the first time around.

FRIENDSHIP

It's not unusual for an Aquarius to marry their best friend, and their partner must at least be in their top three besties to last longer than a millisecond. That means this combo might work better as a friendship, where they can dip in and out. It also flows well if one is the parent and the other is the child, but even then, the results may be disturbing for the Cancer, who desires security and routine. That's annoying for the Aquarius, who feels constantly scrutinized and as a result, makes major mistakes and unfathomable decisions under that pressure.

The Aquarius couldn't be the stay-at-home-baking-cookies type if their lives depended on it. The Cancer loves the smell of home baking, so they may need to excel in the kitchen themselves, hire a chef, or find a stand-in mom (i.e., a nanny).

The Cancer likes to know (and discuss) what is happening in the lives of everyone, which the Aquarius deems meddling. The Cancer finds the Aquarius obtuse, disconcertingly blunt, and at times even pious, which makes innocent bystanders wonder how, and why, these two got together in the first place.

This match can be interesting for wave makers and exciting for lunar babies, but chill it's not. The Cancer is traditional, and the Aquarius isn't keen on convention, especially when the odds are stacked against it anyway. They don't see the logic—and if logic is missing, they tend to zone out. Unless they gravitate more toward responsible Saturn, their old-school ruler, the Aquarius can be as unpredictable as thunder and lightning. Until they get a handle on that voltage, they can cause instability and utter chaos, which will never sit well with their security-loving Cancer.

At least there will never be a dull moment.

REACHING NIRVANA

Overall, kindness for each other and not holding on to grudges is the way for this pairing to work.

There are a few things they *do* have in common: one is unpredictability. It runs throughout the whole of a wave maker's being and is the Cancer's moods 'and feelings. The other commonality is their hearts. They both have a kind and pure heart, which each can take care of for the other, given half the chance. With patience and perseverance, they can build something rather amazing, but the Cancer must stop reacting too quickly and take time to hear where the wave maker's head is. As for the wave makers, they need to try to see the Cancer's demands not as oppression, but as an opportunity for them to share their generosity of spirt and loving-kindness.

If you are a Cancer who loves an Aquarius, contemplate the following:

✧ What is it that attracts you to your lover?

✧ Does this union excite you?

✧ How is your communication in this relationship? Are you open? Or do you internalize?

If you are an Aquarius who loves a Cancer, contemplate the following:

✧ Do you consider yourself compassionate?

✦ Does this union magnify or restrict the above?

✦ Do you need to work on your patience and tolerance? If so, this union ought to help you with that.

Scorpio–Gemini
RULED BY MARS/PLUTO AND MERCURY

When a Gemini comes across a Scorpio, peculiar things happen. They are challenged to review the way they perceive people and relationships in general. It is rarely instant attraction or love at first sight, but more like a chance encounter or forced introduction where they must sit next to each other at a dinner party. The Gemini does recognize early that this hypnotic being has far more going on than meets the eye, which fascinates them. They are sharp and clever, if not a tad arrogant, in their ability to judge people and situations quickly, and the Scorpio is as unpredictable as they are.

As for the Scorpio, they are compelled to explore some form of intimacy with this gloriously airy person who has so many personalities that the chances of getting bored are slim. In that respect, they both have a similar fear of the dull tedium of monotony.

However, the Scorpio, unless they gravitate more toward Aries or Leo in their natal charts, is on a hunt for a soul mate; they have little interest in fleeting affairs. The Gemini finds this concept intriguing, although devotion to them is only ever a novelty, so they just may jump in—after all, what is the worst that can happen? It's not that they don't see the danger lurking beneath the Scorpio's soulful eyes and magnetic energy; they just don't care, and they are not afraid. Power plays and manipulation will be like water off a duck's back: inconsequential.

The Scorpio cannot penetrate through to the soul of a twin because, unless they have Cancer, Scorpio, or a woke sign like Aquarius in their natal charts, the twin isn't attuned to their own higher mind and resides in their monkey-mind of chatter, activity, and trivia. The Scorpio can't find what simply isn't there, which renders them powerless and baffled, yet secretly relieved. What they see is what they get. And how refreshing that is for one who is always having to play human chess, reading between the lines, looking for double meanings and secret enemies. Even when they do lash out at the Gemini, this airy one is far too busy to notice, so the snipes eventually stop and a sort of peace sets in.

FAITHFUL

The Gemini is on a constant search for stimulation, which can cause all sorts of issues for this relationship. They can come across as available and flirtatious, or even be unfaithful, and if Scorpio catches wind of that, they are unlikely to stay. They may get even, but they won't accept their twin's bad behavior for long. This is in stark contrast to how the Gemini deals with the scorpion's infidelity; they rarely feel the need to leave. They may gleefully even the score, but on the whole, they tend to brush off this type of behavior (unless they have Scorpio or Cancer signs in their charts; if the latter is a Moon, Venus, or Mars sign, they will only remain for the sake of financial security, status, the family, or the house). When the Scorpio becomes jealous, the Gemini cannot fathom the reasoning nor logic behind it.

The Scorpio is super private. The Gemini is discreet with their own information but slack with anyone else's, so if their loose lips dare to reveal anything that belonged to the Scorpio, any trust may as well have its own tombstone.

REACHING NIRVANA

The Scorpio needs to be real in terms of what they expect from the Gemini. They will only change if they want to, not because they are forced to, which is an unspoken air sign rule (except for Libra). If the Gemini wishes this union to last, they are going to have to become a lot more unavailable to others and devoted to their lover.

Overall, the intensity and superficiality can be met in the middle, and both can learn and grow. As with all unions, a spiritual belief or practice will allow them to rise above their own animalistic desires and form something incredible.

If you are a Scorpio who loves a Gemini, contemplate the following:

✧ What do you love about your twin?

✧ What is your interpretation of devotion?

✧ Do you have spiritual beliefs?

If you are a Gemini who loves a Scorpio, contemplate the following:

✧ Does your lover excite you? If so, why?

◈ What is the longest relationship you've had? What were the positives?

◈ Do you appreciate your lover's need for loyalty?

◈ Is your Scorpio ever jealous? Do you help them overcome this?

Scorpio–Libra
RULED BY MARS/PLUTO AND VENUS

For these two to attract each other for long enough to form something that resembles a relationship, it's likely that each will have a small dose of the other's sign in their full chart. Otherwise, they are just too different for anything to last more than a week. Without a little of the sexy side of Scorpio, a Libra is too sweet and trusting for a Scorpio. This doesn't mean they are not good enough; it's actually the other way around: the Scorpio believes this gracious child of Venus to be *too* good, and that's the issue. The Scorpio can be conscientious yet submerged in self-loathing and insecurity, which results in them believing that they don't really deserve anyone as honorable as the Libra, or to even be happy. They try to protect their Libra from their worst tendencies, but both possess equal amounts of light and dark and many other commonalities, or there would be no mutual attraction at all.

SEDUCTION

Like a moth to a flame, the Libra is drawn to this unattainable bad boy/girl/gender-fluid human and cannot fathom why their cool beauty and charms are invisible to the Scorpio. They may partake in a brief romance, but the protective nature of the scorpion will kick in and they will leave a rather forlorn Libra in their wake. If, and only if, the Libra has embraced a little of their own Plutonian darkness will they see them as fair game. For the Libra, it's all hands on deck as they attempt to seduce the Scorpio, which is a real challenge because the Scorpio is wary of any emotion that threatens to take away their control, even for one second.

The Scorpio can struggle with obsession, and it's like a stuck record as they replay over and over again just how and why a lover left them. Rarely do they mourn for love like the Libra.

REACHING NIRVANA

For these two beings to be able to form a lasting love, neither can resort to their usual games.

The Libra must be patient and work toward building trust, which will coax the Scorpio out of the fear zone and into their arms. Honesty is crucial, too. The Libra is prone to reflect what they think the Scorpio wants and then become that, which isn't sustainable. Being true to themselves will awaken a respect, and love may then grow over time.

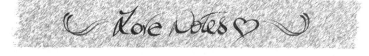

If you are a Scorpio who loves a Libra, contemplate the following:

✧ Do you take time to get to know your lover before making promises?

✧ Are you prone to playing games? If so, why? Is it fear or mischief?

✧ Have you discussed what your needs are in this union? Are they likely to be met?

✧ What do you love about your Libra?

If you are a Libra who loves a Scorpio, contemplate the following:

✧ Are you happy to be yourself from the start of this union?

✧ Do you listen to what your lover wants in this union?

✧ Have you ever used sex to try to win love?

✧ Do you express your own needs?

Scorpio–Aquarius

RULED BY MARS/PLUTO AND SATURN/URANUS

The water bearer and scorpion are magnetized to each other, drawn like bees to pollen—except that some people are allergic to pollen. When these two combine, it can result in either the sweetest honey or a major anaphylactic reaction. They are as similar as they are different. Their Sun signs are what's known as "square," which is when two signs on the zodiac wheel are 90 degrees apart (or three signs away), forming a "hard angle." And with squares, something or someone needs to change to progress. The trouble is, both are fixed and stubborn, always thinking they are right and the other must do the work.

That said, their chemistry is as tangible as the tension. Imagine a rubber band being pulled in two directions with equal force. It will eventually snap. One may assume that the Aquarius would lose this titanic clash, but that wouldn't be a safe bet.

It's not easy being a Scorpio, for even those who try to dim their spotlights and dull their stingers are feared on some level or kept at arm's length. Luckily, Aquarians are not fearful by nature so they find the darkness of Pluto-ruled natives intoxicating. The Scorpio is hypnotized by the light possessed by the Aquarius, and the rest, as they say, is history. Except that no matter how diplomatic relations are to begin with, if one or both is unevolved, a secret war zone may be simmering, with neither truly able to win or destroy the other. This results in a mighty intergalactic fight between the forces of dark and light. One will leave, probably the Aquarius, who dusts their battle scars with fairy dust and starts over.

SUPERPOWERS

The Scorpio may try to use all of their usual tricks and maneuverers to seduce and win in this relationship, but the Aquarius has x-ray vision and doesn't tend to react to covert power plays. That's not to say that they aren't aware of them. They are born with that switch on and spend their whole lives trying to turn it off, to catch a break. They see everything. And the Scorpio is both delighted and terrified that they have been *seen* yet still loved and desired by the water bearer. That is, unless they commit unforgivable acts, such as relentlessly trying to control or manipulate their lover or, the final nail, betrayal. An Aquarius will forgive almost anything, but betrayal? That's when the ice of the Uranian child forms and allows no way back in from the cold. Equally, for the Scorpio, as a water sign, they may forgive the Aquarius more than any other but, if they rightly or wrongly perceive that trust has been broken, they will ghost the Aquarius or set out to destroy them in some way.

Water signs have no real lasting impact on air signs, though, which can drive Scorpio to back down, question their own sanity, or both. The Aquarius has a secret knack for making people (including themselves) go crazy, but it's rarely intentional. Both like to get beneath the surface: the Scorpio probes while the Aquarius digs for, and detects, truth—both have an amazing BS detector—which makes them a formidable team, especially if they work in intelligence or investigative journalism. (Think of Jean Grey, of the X-Men, with her telekinetic and telepathic powers, as an Aquarian.) That's why this union can be both exciting and dangerous in equal measure.

REACHING NIRVANA

For this union to endure the tests of time and the plays for power, both parties need to be self-aware and brutally honest. This is easy for the Aquarius and less so for the Scorpio, who is not always aware of their subconscious drivers. If both become compassionate, retain a sense of humor, and remind each other what they love, all will be well.

The chemistry rarely fizzles out, but sexual compatibility isn't enough to reach nirvana. Spiritual practice is a path toward enlightenment because they both may need to work on their desire and attachments. Yet with their dark and light combined, they have the power to shine like the radiance of gods.

If you are a Scorpio who loves an Aquarius, contemplate the following:

✧ Do you try to control your lover? Be honest. If yes, why? What are you afraid of?

✧ Do you appreciate your partner? If so, what does that look like?

✧ Do you see your own flaws and qualities?

If you are an Aquarius who loves a Scorpio, contemplate the following:

✧ Are you able to see your lover's unique contribution to your life as a blessing?

✧ Do you purposely poke your scorpion for a reaction?

✧ Can you empathize with your lover's jealousy and try to help them overcome this?

Pisces–Gemini
RULED BY JUPITER/NEPTUNE AND MERCURY

If you are familiar with *Winnie-the-Pooh*'s Eeyore and Piglet, you may have some insight into this coupling. Eeyore is pessimistic, like the Pisces, the masochist, all *woe is me*. Piglet, meanwhile, is this sparky being who more than makes up for their lack of common sense with an ever-ready supply of energy and spoken word(s). They don't like to stop moving or talking in case reality takes the opening to rudely enter. The Pisces is often a dreamer, and for this reason, they tend to condone the Gemini's make-believe life, acting with empathy. However, in this union, it will be the fish who eventually forces the twin to get real, which either can be great or not so gratefully accepted, depending on where the twin is in their journey. This love match can help both signs grow and flourish if they are prepared to make some changes to accommodate the other.

The evolved twin is bright, optimistic, open to learning, and trusting, but the unevolved shadow side of that is deceitful, noncommittal, and prone to gaslighting. In short, they use their skilled tongue, mind, and general busyness to deflect blame, dissuade the truth, and dismay the unprepared Pisces into a state of total disarray.

CALM

The Gemini is on a constant search for something. What that is, they are unlikely to know, but with the fish, they are offered a chance to slow down, to be present, and to fall in love. If the fish has the patience to handle this, they have the opportunity to build a rather lovely life, overflowing with mutual interests and possibly even enjoy more creative ways of living. The Gemini in full, positive flow is a marvel, so smart and interesting and curious about everything their love and life have to offer. However, if they are ungrounded, it forever will be impossible to reach the calm waters that fish require from time to time. So the twin must accept that they need to consider their lover's differences and adapt accordingly. It's important that the twin realize how disconcerting their erratic mental and physical activities are for the fish. If they care enough to try to make this union work, compromise is required of both parties.

REACHING NIRVANA

The Gemini keeps moving due to fear, boredom, or worse: being perceived as boring. When they grow emotionally, they can slow down and face themselves, which is endearing to the wise fish who heals and soothes their fears in ways no other has or can.

Fish fall in love with the Gemini mind and their childlike sense of awe at the possibilities life has to offer, but they can be perceived as moody or grumpy and push for their own way. Gemini are also used to getting their way, usually because they exhaust others into submission with their mental agility and hecticness because it's just easier. To reach the sort of enduring love both of them dream of, compromise and communication are called for. The Gemini doesn't like these sorts of real talks, but from time to time, they are required to redress the imbalances and misunderstandings that will undoubtedly arise and threaten to engulf them both, causing rifts in the union.

Accepting their own flaws and appreciating the other's qualities will ensure this union's long-term success.

If you are a Pisces who loves a Gemini, contemplate the following:

✧ Are you patient and compassionate?

✧ Does your twin fascinate you?

✧ Are you creative? If yes, great. If not, please review this because it is self-healing.

✧ Do you understand your lover? If not, do you try?

✧ Can you compromise?

If you are a Gemini who loves a Pisces, contemplate the following:

✧ Are you always on the move? If yes, why?

✧ What would happen if you slowed down? Can you sit quietly? Have you tried to meditate?

✧ Are you critical?

✧ Do you appreciate your fish? Can you list their qualities?

Pisces–Libra
RULED BY JUPITER/NEPTUNE AND VENUS

This has all the makings of a fairy-tale romance, with notes of love that inspire haunting songs and tales that writers embellish for the screen. It *is* like that . . . at first.

A Libra loves to be romanced, and a Pisces is fundamentally romantic. Even fish who have been overpowered by earth planets in their full chart are known to acquiesce, organizing candlelit rooftop diners for two, secret trips, and bathtubs filled with petals for their Libran beauty.

On the surface, this is a harmonious partnership. Both signs tend to prefer peace, beauty, and calm, but if they need to get a little deeper, problems may arise. A Pisces is fine when speaking conceptually, but they are not fans of real talk (unless they have fire or earth Moons or rising signs, etc.), and they find the Libra's incessant need to talk things over and clear stuff up frustrating and, eventually, boring. As for the Libra, they just want to solidify the union and iron out any issues that may be swerving the relationship off course—*their* course.

The Libra is bossy and often the leader in this match. The best way for them to make this, or any other, union work long term is to face what *is* and work with that, rather than trying to mold another person to fit their ideals, which are too high anyway. An obsession with ideals can prevent them from seeing the potential directly in front of them.

ART FORMS
Many often forget that Libra is a logic-driven air sign underneath their poetic and "peace and love for all" exterior, and in their flow,

there is no sign as fair and just. Their charm and diplomacy (unless they have a Sagittarius Moon or rising sign) is irresistible, which readily makes people feel valued, cared for, and listened to. They don't like gossip and will quickly leave the room or shut down the perpetrator and inform the injured party of any salacious chatter, all in the sake of fairness. When the Pisces witnesses this uncontrived goodness, they fall in love, truly, madly, and deeply. This Libra marvel has the potential to reignite the ingrained Pisces faith in the goodness of people, life, love, humanity, and the universe.

In return, the Libra is enchanted by the gentle strength of the fish, their innate creativity, and their artisan soul. They feel at peace and at home, perceiving them to be their soul mate and as close to perfection as they have ever encountered.

There are a few exceptions to the rule: a Pisces loves and appreciates art, as does a Libra, but even when a Libra's beauty may rival that of Nefertiti's, if they are one of those rare unevolved beings who cares little for others and only for how the world perceives them, or if they have failed to educate themselves, it wouldn't matter if they resemble Venus herself—a Pisces will swim away fast.

REACHING NIRVANA

A Libra requires balance, which means they are prepared to see every side of everything. If a Pisces accepts this, they won't feel judged or as if their lover has refused to stand by them.

Fish require calm, tranquil waters to be able to gather their thoughts and heal from life in general, and a Libra must not take this as a slight against them.

If both can accept how things are and not try to change each other, compromise will naturally arise.

Focusing on their common interests is a failproof way to form a new life that encompasses them both.

If you are a Pisces who loves a Libra, contemplate the following:

✧ What attracted you to your Libra? List the qualities here.

✧ Are you able to address any imbalances in this relationship?

✧ Do you both appreciate the arts? How can you make this more of a combined pastime?

If you are a Libra who loves a Pisces, contemplate the following:

✧ Do you accept your lover as they are?

✧ What does your ideal relationship look like, and what does that mean for this one?

✧ Do you educate yourself? What books have you read that may have opened your mind?

✧ What is peace to you? Does this union bring you peace?

Pisces–Aquarius

RULED BY JUPITER/NEPTUNE AND SATURN/URANUS

This is a meeting of creative and spiritually inclined souls or minds, depending on your beliefs or nonbeliefs. Either way, whether this is a friendship or a romance, sparks of ingenuity will fly, creative ideas are likely to pour forth, and new inventions will be imagined. Both of these extraordinary beings have plenty to offer each other, and indeed the world, and the potential to achieve so much together.

Fish are escape artists by nature and naturally inclined to using their imaginations to flee from an otherwise mundane worldly life. An Aquarius will wriggle like Houdini to flee a cage, too. Neither can quite believe that they have managed to find such a willing and equally skilled partner with whom to skip through life, laughing in the face of conformity.

A Pisces needs plenty of alone time to gather their thoughts and relax, and an Aquarius suffers if they're constantly bombarded with information and energy, so they will happily give each other space.

Unless the Aquarius is the Saturn-ruled, down-to-earth, serious type, or the Pisces has institutionalized themselves in some regular nine-to-five job or other empirical construct because they need routine, these two are a match made in some undefinable cosmos one may call heaven.

This all sounds idyllic, but as with any union, there are issues, particularly between their water and air natures. An Aquarius is blunt and, in their full-throttle mode, care nothing for the opinions or thoughts of others. The fish would like to be this way, but they are sensitive to the feelings and emotions of others and find their air sign friend or lover disconcertingly rude, which causes feathers (or scales) to ruffle.

TRUST

Fish in their flow are honest and trustworthy, but we also have the slippery type their sign is known for. They lack boundaries and say whatever they need to in order to continue doing what they like. Now, Aquarius can't work with the latter because they consider themselves open-minded enough to renegotiate the terms and conditions if they are not fair for all. If the fish lies or attempts to deceive the wave maker, then all hell breaks loose, mainly because the Aquarius is outraged that the fish underestimated their pervasive psychic skills and penetrating telepathy. Insulting the intuition and intelligence of a wave maker is the worst thing you can do. Their ego will fight 'til the death. The fish will resort to playing the victim, and no matter how hard they try to make amends, unless they fully confess their conscious (and subconscious) moves to outwit or out-maneuver their Aquarius, then it's over, as the airy one brings down the gavel of judgment with their fixed and firm hand. If they deduce that this fish is not to be trusted, both may as well call it quits. This shocks the fish beyond belief because they have never been caught quite so spectacularly before and they wonder where the kind and compassionate being they used to know went. The Aquarius is gone with the wind, leaving a real void. After the mourning period, though, the fish is usually relieved to have some peace back in their life. (But both will secretly miss each other.)

REACHING NIRVANA

A joint creative hobby or project bonds these two and helps them create a magical world away from the mundanities of regular living, which soothes them both.

Respecting each other's differences is key to achieving better harmony and less friction, but this will only happen when the fish is protective, not reactive, and the wave maker is considerate and patient—the latter is a lifelong lesson for an Aquarius. Fish are patient with life but not necessarily people, and for the wave maker, it's the other way around, so the middle ground is the best place for these two signs to meet.

If you are a Pisces who loves an Aquarius, contemplate the following:

✧ Are you honest with your Aquarius?

✧ Do you explain that you need quiet time alone?

✧ Do you explain your needs and express your feelings? This helps your Aquarius because they veer toward pure logic.

If you are an Aquarius who loves a Pisces, contemplate the following:

✧ What do you love about your fish? Do you tell them?

✧ Are you a considerate lover?

✧ Do you share interests? What are they?

✧ Does your fish trigger your compassion?

Earth and Air Signs Combined
Taurus–Gemini
RULED BY VENUS/GAIA AND MERCURY

The bull and the twin can't help the initial attraction. It burns so brightly that they may even move heaven and earth (and current partners) to form a union.

Because these signs are next to each other on the zodiac wheel, it's likely that they both have a little of the other's sign in their full chart, which helps them understand and tolerate each other. If not, the Taurus is more likely to get annoyed with the Gemini and their contrary nature, and the Gemini may decide that they can't settle down with someone as fixed and opiniated. In that case, the Gemini will probably hop into another relationship rather quickly (unless they have Mars or Moon in Taurus), and the Taurus will need to partake in a silent retreat for a few months to decompress.

The Taurus usually delights in the Gemini. They live their life in completely different ways, always open to new possibilities and ready to take risks in the name of fun, and that's invigorating for this earth bull who can't seem to avoid getting stuck in ruts or dragged down by monotony. It can be marvelous, but it can also cause chaos, which either drives the sensible and pragmatic bull mad with lust and desire or insane with the tension of it all. Perhaps both.

LIGHTNESS

The Taurus looks upon the Gemini with love and affection. They help them laugh and lighten up. Bulls are often so weighed down by responsibility and their sense of duty is so strong that their Gemini is like a breath of cool air on a stuffy day. For this respite, they are willing to commit in ways they may never have felt safe enough to do before. This Venus-ruled beauty offers the Gemini loyalty and steadfast support, which makes the twin feel supported and appreciated, and also shares their sensuality that's combined with a natural goodness. Like the scent of flowers blooming in the summer, to the Gemini, it's utterly intoxicating.

REACHING NIRVANA

For this union to thrive and endure, both must take time to understand how the other relaxes. Bulls need downtime and so do twins, but only the evolved among them know that. Spending time in the natural beauty of Mother Earth grounds the Gemini and rejuvenates both of their souls.

Sensuality is important for the Taurus, and if the Gemini is open to learning new ways of intimacy, then all will be well.

Bulls will skip from adventure to adventure with their Gemini, but only if they feel that their Gemini compromises and that all is fair and equal in their lives.

The twin needs to slow down and face themselves rather than running as fast as they can. When they finally attune to the gentle voice of their soul, they will feel more complete than ever before. Bulls are all about the soul, so together, and with enough patience and gentle communication, they can make this last.

If you are a Taurus who loves a Gemini, contemplate the following:

✧ Does your twin fascinate you? If so, tell them!

✧ Do you feel that there is enough compromise between you?

✧ How do you relax? Watching television doesn't count because it's a stimulant.

✧ Do you ever give each other sensual massages? If not, try it.

If you are a Gemini who loves a Taurus, contemplate the following:

✧ Do you slow down for long enough to look into your lover's eyes and connect to their soul?

✧ Does your bull give the best hugs? I bet they do!

✧ Are you willing to learn how to become more sensual, without rushing?

✧ Feeding bulls is important, as is getting them out in nature, but they also need down time. Do you provide that for your bull?

Taurus–Libra

RULED BY VENUS/GAIA AND VENUS

This superb love match has all the right ingredients to give both people exactly what they want and need. Both share the same ruling planet, Venus, and have equal amounts of her goddess vibes and sparkle that they can bestow on each other.

The Taurus is often the earthier and more pragmatic of the two, but they also are likely to have as much charm and grace of spirit as the Libra. Unless the Taurus has a strong planet misbehaving in Gemini (in their full natal charts), they are dependable and private, which suits the Libra well. Neither enjoys gossip or sharing their personal lives with anyone outside their inner circle, which, in a world filled with loose lips, makes them feel like kindred spirits, confident enough to open their hearts and reveal their souls to each other.

SHARED VALUES

At heart, both signs are quietly traditional and have shared values in that respect, which means that affairs are not likely and that both will strive to build an honest and solid relationship. The only drawback may be for the Taurus, who will expect total dedication. If the scales is truly ready for this, it's fine; if not, jealousy or resentment may rear its ugly head. If that happens, the Libra will begin to lose affection, so the Taurus needs rest safe in the knowledge that they are enough.

The Libra often has such high ideals that it's hard for *them* to live up to them, let alone another human. It's much more advisable for the Libra to try to live in the moment, accept how wonderful life is, and realize how much their heart glows when another being as special as their Taurus accepts them.

REACHING NIRVANA

For both to flourish, they must work on their levels of attachment to outdated modes of behavior or goals and let go of their need to control every aspect of the life they have together, reviewing their perceptions of what a flawless partnership looks like. There is no such thing. Compromise is what's called for, and if they weigh (good for the scales to help with this one) what works and what can be negotiated, all will be well.

If you are a Taurus who loves a Libra, contemplate the following:

✧ Is this union harmonious? If yes, great. If not, what can you do to address this?

✧ Do you suffer with attachment issues? If so, try to explore why and what can be done to lessen them, which will help you become more contented.

✧ Do you and your Libra communicate with ease?

If you are a Libra who loves a Taurus, contemplate the following:

✧ Do you have high ideals and expectations? If yes, write them down and then contemplate how many are realistic and how many are currently being met.

✧ What does your ideal partner look like? How much of this is reflected in your Taurus?

✧ Are you able to compromise in a balanced way so it feels equal?

Taurus–Aquarius
RULED BY VENUS/GAIA AND SATURN/URANUS

If bulls have ever been bored in a previous relationship, the universe heard those wails and sent in an Aquarius, with a flash of thunder and more than a few lightning bolts. There will never be a dull moment with these two, that's for sure.

This union generally starts in a peculiar fashion. It's rare for a bull and a wave maker to meet in an ordinary way, which is often why the bull is lured into wanting to know more. Even though they quickly become aware of the fact that this being walks a fine line between crazy and undeniable genius, that is the test. If you converse for more than twenty minutes and nothing random pops up, then you aren't speaking to a true wave maker, unless they have a ton of Virgo or Capricorn in their full charts or have determined to hide in plain sight. However, these folks are not known to hide. They care little for the opinions of other people, and unless they have Cancer planets, they are secure and confident in their "crazy," with enough friends who accept them, so they don't need to worry about a relative stranger's take. To bulls, this cool confidence is like catnip to felines: addictive, irresistible, and irrational.

All of this is somewhat calmer or less pronounced if the Aquarius happens to have a Moon/Mars/Venus or rising sign in Taurus in their full charts. If the Taurus has at least one luminary in

Aquarius, they may not quite feel as though this new love has beamed in from outer space.

The bull in full flow has a cool demeanor that's uber-attractive to the wave maker. They are strong (check) and brave (double check), and when they are confident enough, they don't worry about the opinions of others yet are still kind and loving (check, check, check). If a bull is all of the above and also comfortable in their own skin, the Aquarius will be all in.

DOUBLE O

This relationship starts with fascination. The Aquarius is often aloof and hard to read, which beguiles the bull. But when they connect, the result is a passion that transforms into the deepest love either may have encountered. Its growth will be steady, but also very new to both, and neither will quite know how to handle it.

There is likely to be much storming off, tantrums, breakups, and stand-offs. Both are fixed signs, and bulls certainly have met their match in the stubborn department. They share a "double O" nature: one is obtuse, and the other is obstinate. Although some awful bullish behavior may be greeted with a wry smile, a clever or funny comment, or the patience of a saint, other offenses will be furiously challenged. You can never quite be sure of what will offend the Uranian-born. It's rarely what the bull thinks will goad a reaction, but when they get angry, thunder claps and lightning crackles, and that's just it. The bull might be flabbergasted, but still in awe that this coolheaded person can be so unpredictable. They possess just as much fury and are able to keep their partner in check when necessary, with enough heart to truly love them at the same time.

If the communication stops, the relationship probably will come to an end. Bulls get tired, and wave makers are easily bored. But it is more likely that the making up will more than compensate for the chaos, and with every bust-up, more understanding and tolerance will arise as they are forced to communicate. This can take a few years (or light-years) to settle down, but when the lines are drawn and the boundaries are set, something steady can set in.

REACHING NIRVANA

When a bull and a wave maker fall in love on a soul level that transcends the purely physical attraction, nothing will break that karmic bond of mutual appreciation and devotion. Both will decide that they can't live without the other, and the storms eventually will subside. There still may be a little harsh wind if the Aquarius detaches for too long or snaps with lightning, or if the Taurus takes their airy lover for granted, but overall, they will start to perform as a dynamic duo.

Bulls must be fit so they don't become too fixed in their bodies or minds, and the Aquarius ought to exercise to stay grounded. So healthy regimes are important to both, as is mindfulness and anything that can expand the mind.

If you are a Taurus who loves an Aquarius, contemplate the following:

✧ Do you lose your temper easily? How can you prevent that and still be heard?

✧ Are you "seen" and understood by your lover? If yes, do you offer the same to them?

✧ How do you maintain this union?

✧ Do you listen to your partner?

✧ What is their favorite pastime?

Love Notes

If you are an Aquarius who loves a Taurus, contemplate the following:

✧ Do you appreciate your bull's values? What are they?

✧ Is this union balanced, with give and take?

✧ What do you love about your bull?

✧ Do you feel "seen"?

✧ Do you "see" them?

Virgo–Gemini
RULED BY MERCURY/CHIRON AND MERCURY

The virgin and the twin share a ruling planet, which is probably as much as they will ever be inclined to divvy up, unless the Virgo has a wonderful sense of humor and the Gemini wears some lead in the heels of their tap shoes. Without any air or fire to lighten them up, virgins have little to no chance of surviving this relationship with their fragile egos intact, and the Gemini may even have visible slices where the Virgo's razor-sharp tongue cut deep. This is what is known as a "squared" union, which is when two signs are three spaces apart on the zodiac wheel. Imagine two stags sizing each other up, just about to lock antlers in battle. That's what a squared union is like, except it doesn't end in a major clash.

Both come together to learn and, hopefully, grow into better versions of themselves. Both are on Earth to learn how to communicate, which involves listening more than talking, so they tend to learn from their partner just how *not* to be, which is great if it's all done in the name of love. If they stay together, it would mean that the Virgo has loosened up and the Gemini has tightened up. The twin just wants to have fun, but if the Virgo won't play with them, that's fine, too. They will go through their contacts to find someone who may be up for a gathering—anything other than tidying up the mess they left behind for the Virgo to clean up. If the Virgo dares to question them, they will protest that they are being controlling and fly out of the room like a wailing gust of wind, leaving the Virgo to tidy up (again) and wait patiently for the dust to settle. If this union is balanced with give and take, the stars shine on them both. If it goes wrong, the Virgo becomes as cold as ice and the Gemini will rebel by emotionally ghosting the Virgo and eventually physically disappearing.

If the Gemini gets frustrated, they may throw temper tantrums or lash out with spiteful statements to stop an imagined or real virgin attack, which the Virgo mostly shrugs off unless they have a Cancer or Scorpio Venus/Moon or rising sign, in which case they will hold that hurt forever and commit to psychological payback with cruel comments at home and in public as well as constant criticism. A war of words and a fight for control may ensue if they close their hearts to each other.

COMMUNICATION

Neither is particularly skilled when it comes to knowing their audience or reading a room (unless either has Aquarius, Scorpio, or Pisces planets). The Gemini may hurt people's feelings because they don't always engage their brain before saying whatever is on their mind. The same can be said for the Virgo. The two tease each other, put up their hands to ask permission to take over the stage and speak, and take turns being the grown-up. There is something childlike about them both that draws them together and keeps them hanging on to each other's every word, for decades.

They both can be critical, but if they each keep their heart open and bite their lip before they say something hurtful or demeaning, it will trigger their brain to remind them of all the reasons they love their partner, healing them immensely. Saying something kind instead of something close to mean is the most powerful heart-opener of all. It is truly the most beautiful of gifts, both for the giver and the receiver.

REACHING NIRVANA

The Gemini is funny, whip-smart, and amusing. The Virgo is super-smart, too—a little less forthcoming with the belly laughs and grandiose declarations, but humorous nevertheless. As long as lightness prevails, this love will grow and blossom like an eternal spring.

They must watch out for any tit-for-tat behavior and always try to work on a healthy balance of give and take, speaking their truth with love and without blame. This will help them prevent catastrophic misunderstandings along the way.

If you are a Virgo who loves a Gemini, contemplate the following:

✧ What are your biggest fears? Do you know what your lover's fears are?

✧ Are you aware of, and sensitive to, your partner's needs?

✧ How do you resolve disputes or arguments with your lover?

✧ Are you forgiving?

If you are a Gemini who loves a Virgo, contemplate the following:

✧ Do you listen to your partner?

✧ Are you emotionally mature?

✧ Instead of criticizing your lover or the relationship, try loving-kindness instead. (This will trigger the "being in love" feeling for you, too.)

✧ Do you feel loved? How does that make you feel?

✧ How do you create intimacy and build trust?

Virgo–Libra
RULED BY MERCURY/CHIRON AND VENUS

When the virgin and the scales chance upon one another, the sun shines on them both. This partnership has success and longevity written all over it.

It's been so hard for them, being so perfect in such an imperfect world, and when they gaze into each other's eyes, the angels sing. Well, that is until the Virgo realizes that the Libra snores and the Libra sees that the Virgo isn't always quite as "together" as they claim to be. The Virgo *is* often the tidiest person on Earth, but at other times, their home can look like it was recently ransacked.

The Virgo appreciates the Libra's diplomacy (unless they have fire sign planets in their full charts) and logic, which is evenly optimistic and balances the virgin's tendency to be a tad pessimistic. They do not, however, take kindly to the extravagant Libra, and even if all the scales' rent money was spent on a gift for them, it will cause much chagrin.

Their compatibility is particularly obvious if the Virgo has planets, such as Moon, Mars, or Venus, or a rising sign in Libra and vice versa, Saturn in the sign, or a connection by a trine (a favorable astrological aspect that forms when two people's planets connect via a 120 degree angle in a natal chart) or sextile (a spark that occurs when one person's planet connects to the other's via a 60 degree angle). Although the Saturn connections give a relationship a star stamp of approval and the impetus for a couple to stay committed, the latter shows where the person's restrictions lie, as well as any karmic lessons to be learned in respect to the sign it falls under. This may cause issues to flare up so they can be resolved once and for all. In fact, it's rare for the virgin and scales to form any kind of serious union without complementary planets in each other's signs.

SELF-IMPROVEMENT

This earth and air sign association provides a good balance, which is a requisite for the Libra and Virgo to be able to coexist. Although nobody really talks about the virgin's need for balance, it is an astro fact. Their starry formation sings a symphony only they can hear. It truly is a wonderful match, especially if both face themselves for long enough to develop their own levels of self-awareness and if they are evolving (or at least trying to).

The Virgo in their flow is constantly working on something, and if their paid work dries up, they start working on themselves, which is usually why the universe forces the well to run dry at times so they can reflect and turn the focus on themselves and their lives.

The Libra is often wise, but only when they get a little older. When that happens, they have intelligence equal to the virgin's.

REACHING NIRVANA

If this union began with a bang, or a night of passion, it's not likely to last as long as it otherwise could. This relationship requires time to marinate so trust can be built and respect can be earned. When the two truly get to know each other, as opposed to just reflecting each other's fabulous qualities, they will realize that this relationship has the potential they both secretly hoped it would.

It's helpful if both share a similar faith and practice spirituality together. Otherwise, they may argue over whose version of God or the universe is the correct one or what the point of life may be.

If you are a Virgo who loves a Libra, contemplate the following:

✧ Do you romance your lover?

✧ How did this union begin? What was the initial attraction?

✧ Are you able to relax together?

If you are a Libra who loves a Virgo, contemplate the following:

✧ Are you and your lover similar? In what ways?

✧ What common interests do you have?

✧ Do you accept your lover? Or do you try to change them to fit your ideals?

Virgo–Aquarius
RULED BY MERCURY/CHIRON AND SATURN/URANUS

The virgin meets the wave maker, which translates to sense and rebellion combined, and this can go either way. Sensible rebellions are always preferable to virgins, and if it has some real purpose that serves a greater good, they will get behind it—but only after serious thought, overanalysis, and procrastination.

As clever and logical as an Aquarius can be, they are also as random as it gets. Now, a Virgo can appreciate randomness because it's required to test and speed up algorithms—that, they can understand. But the wave maker's brand of random? They cannot fathom any reason for such unpredictable and unsettling displays in an otherwise perfectly reasonable human being. The average Aquarius easily lulls the poor and unsuspecting virgin into a false sense of security and into believing this equally clever and wise air sign is a kindred spirit. Then, whoosh! They do or say something that renders the Virgo speechless—which is a small miracle because virgins are known for never missing a beat with their clever replies and brutal honesty.

ASSETS

I use the word *poor* in association with the Virgo in a union with an Aquarius both lightly and in jest. What I mean is "long suffering." I feel the need to explain this word association for both signs, simply because it gives me the opportunity to explain one of the characteristics these two share: the Aquarius takes *every* word literally, unless accompanied by a whole host of explanatory emojis or suitable grammar, such as several exclamation marks. To the analytical Virgo, it is much the same; they are economical with words unless they are trying to make a point; in that case, they can cause the Aquarian eyes to water. And they choose fact over fiction, every time.

The Virgo is unlikely to be poor in the material sense because they are earnest about creating financial stability and dedicated to holding on to the assets they have. I'm not saying they are tight; more like thrifty.

But being above average on the intelligence scale and taking everything literally is where the similarities end. The Aquarius lives for the moment, and although they spend more time in the future than most, they don't plan for it by saving or accruing assets, which annoys the Virgo, who seems to be the only one intent on saving for a rainy day or for their retirement. Retiring is not something the Aquarius ever plans to do—I mean, who can retire from saving humanity, the planet, and every animal on Earth? Although likely to have suffered many a rainy day due to financial instability, the Aquarius has no real interest in money, which seems disrespectful and irresponsible to the frugal Virgo. Unless the Aquarian was born into it, married a Virgo or Capricorn, or invented something they then sold for billions, it's unlikely that these two ever will agree on how to make, spend, or save money—a major reason for them to butt heads.

Although the Aquarius and their eclectic collections of friends, interests, and pastimes fascinate the virgin at first, in the long run it frazzles their sensibilities, and they may start to long for a quieter life.

REACHING NIRVANA

This is a splendid combination for a friendship, but they will not understand each other as a committed partnership unless they have a sprinkle of each other's sign in their full chart. If both decide that they want to settle into a relationship, their mutual need for control must be relinquished, and honesty and devotion will help them navigate through.

The Aquarius is intuitive, so if they don't read the pages and pages of emails or messages sent, it's okay; they've scanned through and gotten the point. The Virgo needs to accept how things are, and the Aquarius must make moves to soothe their virgin's fears with kindness and patience. It will work, but patience needs to be ever present for the love to survive.

If you are a Virgo who loves an Aquarius, contemplate the following:

✧ Try to use logic with kindness with your lover, instead of criticism.

✧ What do you appreciate about your partner? Do you tell them?

✧ Do you attempt to control your lover or their behavior?

✧ Find new ways to express your needs. Take note and then adapt to ways that work.

If you are an Aquarius who loves a Virgo, contemplate the following:

✧ Are you patient and tolerant with your virgin?

✧ Do you rightly or wrongly assume your partner is controlling? Explore this with them.

✧ What do you love about your partner?

✧ If you know your lover suffers from anxiety, what can you do to change how you may trigger this?

Capricorn–Gemini
RULED BY SATURN AND MERCURY

Contrary to a widespread misconception, this is probably one of the best air and earth combinations. Gemini is a mutable sign, which means they will change and adapt according to their environment or who is winning; they'll even change sides, unlike the opinionated version of the Libra, on the other hand, who likes their own way, or a fixed, rebellious Aquarian. Goats prefer the Gemini's mercurial versatility. It means that their airy lover has enough intelligence and sass to keep them interested long term, yet will toe the line and behave when required or if there is something in it for them and it's not necessary for too long. The Gemini has a short attention span because there is so much more out there to excite them, and that's the driver for them. If their lover is deemed exciting, or has a fascinating career and varied transatlantic lifestyle, the Gemini is all in. If the Gemini has an array of Cancer planets, like the Moon, Venus, or Mercury, then and only then is there a chance that they will settle for consistency and stay closer to home.

The Gemini does get caught up or distracted, and when they turn around, any other lover may have given up and be long gone, but not the Capricorn. They are still there, and after this charade has occurred several times, the Gemini will finally stop for long enough to take note. Ah, so maybe, just maybe, this goat is a keeper after all, they say.

Some goats have a zany sense of humor and indulge in spontaneity from time to time, and if so, this is a starry match, but they like to choose if and when that happens.

The Gemini, for the most part, is content to skip off on adventures without warning, and they are not that bothered if it's alone or accompanied. When they realize that their goat doesn't complain about this, they carry on carrying on. This is refreshingly reassuring for them. When the Gemini returns, the goat is glad to see them and vice versa, as long as they have not missed any social engagements. (Goats like to plan and prepare.) The Gemini is delighted not to receive the usual indignance or fury they have faced with other lovers because of their flighty ways.

FUN

Goats like to have fun, as long as it doesn't stand in the way of their work or cause any kind of impediment to them building an empire. The Gemini provides fun and levity in abundance.

The twin is not the type to dissuade any lover from their worldly ambitions; on the contrary, they love nice and shiny things, being rather like magpies in that respect. The more a goat can offer them, the happier they are. You *can* turn a twin's head with designer gifts, fine dining, and exotic holidays, but it wouldn't be enough to make them commit long term. They need continuous mental and physical stimulation.

Goats delight in the diverse Gemini mind and listen earnestly. They even offer sage advice to help their Gemini actualize some of their more sensible ideas. If they do decide to team up, together they build dreams that endlessly inspire both.

Most say that a Capricorn has a strong moral compass and is faithful, and that a Gemini is not, but this isn't always the case. A Capricorn will stray from time to time, and if that happens, you can bet your last dollar it's because they believed the relationship was already on life support. If a lover forgives them, they will soon lose respect, and either way, it ends. In that respect, the Gemini is the same. They cheat if they feel rejected or get bored and think they can get away with it. If they get caught and their partner forgives them, no matter what they may say, they think it's game on and their clandestine love affairs will continue until the goat calls time.

REACHING NIRVANA

Goats must respect their partner, and if that changes, for whatever reason, the union will be short-lived.

If this relationship started as an affair, it's unlikely to last. Goats don't appreciate the humiliation of infidelity, and even if they go all-out to win someone else's partner, they rarely will ever trust their partner when they do triumph. A Gemini must not play mind games but instead should be open and honest.

If these two form a union a little later in life, after both have sampled all that the world has to offer in the guise of other lovers, the match does have the potential to last long term, if not forever.

If both believe in karma and cause and effect, they will be careful with each other and offer a support that no other pairing can even come close to.

If you are a Capricorn who loves a Gemini, contemplate the following:

✧ Do you appreciate your lover's intelligence and humor?

✧ Are you prepared to commit to your lover? If yes, why? If you are not sure, why not?

✧ How does this love match differ from any past unions?

If you are a Gemini who loves a Capricorn, contemplate the following:

✧ What is it that initially attracted you to your lover? Make a list and note how many are still relevant.

✧ Are you both able to laugh together?

✧ Do you respect your lover? If yes, how so? List the reasons.

Capricorn–Libra
RULED BY SATURN AND VENUS

This is undoubtedly the best combination of air and earth because a Libra is pointedly driven to become half of another and a Capricorn perceives relationships to be just like any other commitment, with success firmly rooted in hard work. Goats will work to maintain a relationship, and a Libra is less likely to give up on them than any other air sign. So the union happily chugs along . . . until it doesn't.

The Libra in their full flow of charm, beauty, and intelligence bewitches most folk, but for the Capricorn, their allure is irresistible. They fall in love quickly, and if Libra does, too, then it's a sure bet that they will commit, maybe marry, and stay together through thick and thin. Unless, that is, the Libra is still on the hunt for what they think are the ideal partner and life. Then their expectations are far too high. It's only when they have tired of the various failures in their love life that they may be more open to giving this one a real go.

The evolved Libra is exquisite, light, and graceful and quite unlike any lover the Capricorn has ever encountered, which opens their wary heart to the possibilities of love like flowers just blooming. And goats could almost burst into song at the happiness they feel with their lover. It's magical and seemingly predestined.

Capricorns have their own style of beauty—more classic and refined with rarely a hair out of place—which the Libra appreciates greatly.

COMMITMENT

Goats are very much like their opposite sign, Cancer. They are conservative and have traditional, perhaps old-fashioned views. A Libra *thinks* they are the same, but really they are not. They usually believe in one true love, but Libras who have more feminine energy are especially headstrong, driven to doing things their own way. Goats see right through them because goats don't bend; they command, or demand, or simply state that this is so . . . and it is so. This is where it gets interesting, for both signs. Each truly feels that they have, indeed, met their match and happened upon a yin and yang balance of energies that may just be worthy of a long-term commitment. If the goat and the scales are young, or in different places in their lives with regards to relationships, then the above doesn't come into play. If both are ready to forsake all others, however, this union is likely to stand the tests of time and its distractions.

REACHING NIRVANA

At their best, a Libra is tolerant and amiable and will spend time finding ways to be a better partner, which will make their goat feel valued and prioritized. A Capricorn tends to be the more pragmatic and seemingly bullish force, but their motivations are always sincere and they take the future of the union seriously.

Lightening up and enjoying romance is key for both, or they tend to miss opportunities for enjoying life, their love, and the magic of the moment. When a Libra accepts what is, and is content that the goat will offer the kind of love that supports them, enabling them to explore their lives as a true partnership, the relationship can flourish.

As with all unions, any spiritual practice will help them become better versions of themselves and better lovers. Faith in a higher power gives both a confidence nothing worldly ever could.

If you are a Capricorn who loves a Libra, contemplate the following:

✧ What do you appreciate about your Libra?

✧ Does your lover make you smile?

✧ Does this union bring out the best version of you?

If you are a Libra who loves a Capricorn, contemplate the following:

✧ What initially attracted you to your lover?

✧ Are you able to envision a future together? What does this look like?

✧ Are your ideals aligned with your lover's? Have you checked?

Capricorn–Aquarius
RULED BY SATURN AND SATURN/URANUS

If the goat has a good helping of Aquarius in its full natal chart and the Aquarius has at least one planet in Capricorn, these two are bound to have more in common, certainly have a better chance of understanding each other, and stand a real chance of forming something spectacular. If neither shares in the other's sign, it's unlikely that this pairing will work without leaving the goat feeling as if they've been electrocuted and the Aquarius short-circuiting or having a mighty meltdown as they buckle under the weight of their lover's earthy thumb.

When a goat commits, they do so wholeheartedly. After an Aquarius has observed their potential match from some faraway star, quietly analyzing their qualities and flaws, they, too, will commit. Loyalty is what keeps these two hearts beating in unison, and they give and take trust in equal measure. Wave makers are generally honest with a unique blend of integrity and anarchy, which fascinates the shrewd goat. This union usually works best if the Capricorn is female, or gravitates more toward the feminine energy, because then they are more compassionate and tolerant of their wave maker.

The initial attraction is strong. Goats know, subconsciously, that they have plenty to learn from wave makers. Indeed, they are starred to be born under their sign the next time around, but still, they rebel against that. They have such a reliance on societal approval that they usually end up getting annoyed, or maybe even embarrassed, because their Aquarian rarely cares for "idiotic" rules or the opinions of strangers. They are more concerned with things that they feel really do matter, such as the plight of humanity, the climate, or the number of animals and fish that are slaughtered every day and then just wasted. They care that formal education fails to cultivate individualism, which is imperative for growth and innovation, or the intuitive and creative part of a child's mind, and so forth. You can see why this match is a challenge.

Of course, there are wave makers who slide toward Saturnian

principles, those that align with the goat's modus operandi. If this is the case, the two will form a steady, earthy union that doesn't change much, aside from the living room wallpaper. But that would be a shame, because the wave maker's out-of-the-box and compassionate thought processes are needed. The world requires altruistic and progressive viewpoints now more than ever, as we are experiencing a paradigm shift unlike anything that has been seen since the time of Atlantis. But try telling a goat all that, and they will call in the psychiatrists.

If the goat has their way, their Aquarius will be darning socks and collecting five mini-goats from school every day, which is not what they were born for. That may work for a few years, but the wave maker will rebel spectacularly at some stage, leaving the goat looking, and feeling, electrocuted by the shock.

POWER

If the goat is on the more serious side of Capricorn, they have the power to unwittingly make moves that might suppress the free and wild spirt of their eternal child. Capricorn is duty bound to work for the old guard and support the system, so this relationship is not going to be easy. Unless they both realize that they come from different solar systems and usually have very opposing agendas, they quite easily could cause each other much harm.

If this union is not handled with loving-kindness and tolerance, the two may drive each other crazy. If both are evolved, though, they have the potential to become a power couple who bridge the much-needed gap between the age of Aquarius and the old guard, hell bent on destruction and inequality. For that to happen, a whole lot of mutual respect and love is required. That's a tall order for anyone, but especially for these two.

REACHING NIRVANA

These two are unlikely to create a "normal" or socially acceptable homestead, but they do have the potential to build an unusual and vibrant life. They may make remarkable changes within society that are, thanks to the goat, "acceptable" and reasonable, and courtesy of the Aquarius, progressive and forward-thinking.

Goats in their flow have brilliant, quick minds and delight in their air sign lover's way of thinking and sense of humor. Both are prone to taking themselves too seriously, and if this is the case, the partnership is doomed because lower ego causes a fight for dominance. But if they both possess humor, that's an alchemical process that's destined to bring them both eternal joy and happiness.

This union often works best if both are older and wiser. Again, humor is the key, as is working on their minds with meditation or mindfulness, which will help them sidestep their need to have their own way and forge something else that is based on growth and compromise.

If you are a Capricorn who loves an Aquarius, contemplate the following:

✧ Do you appreciate your lover's quirks?

✧ Are you prone to following the rules? Even when they don't work? List examples.

✧ Can you communicate your needs without becoming critical?

✧ Are you open-minded?

If you are an Aquarius who loves a Capricorn, contemplate the following:

✧ Do you appreciate your goat's wisdom?

✧ Do you force your opinions on your lover? Or are you able to gently open their mind?

✧ Are you able to compromise your need for freedom with commitment?

✧ Are you patient with yourself and your lover?